The Love Drama of C. G. Jung

Marie-Louise von Franz, Honorary Patron

Studies in Jungian Psychology by Jungian Analysts

Daryl Sharp, General Editor

THE LOVE DRAMA OF C. G. JUNG

As Revealed In His Life And In His *Red Book*

Maria Helena Mandacarú Guerra

Translated from Portuguese by Alex Forman

Originally published as *O Livro Vermelho - O Drama de Amor de C .G. Jung.*

Thanks for permissions from W.W. Norton for passages from the *Red Book* and Random House for quotations from *Memories, Dreams, Reflections.*

Library and Archives Canada Cataloguing in Publication

Guerra, M. Helena Mandacarú, 1953-, author
The love drama of C. G. Jung as revealed in his life and in his Red Book / M. Helena Mandacarú Guerra.

(Studies in Jungian psychology by Jungian analysts ; 140)
Includes bibliographical references and index.
ISBN 978-1-894574-42-6 (pbk.)

1. Jung, C. G. (Carl Gustav), 1875-1961. 2. Jung, C. G. (Carl Gustav), 1875-1961. Liber novus. 3. Jung, C. G. (Carl Gustav), 1875-1961--Relations with women. 4. Jung, Emma. 5. Spielrein, Sabina. 6. Wolff, Toni. I. Title. II. Series: Studies in Jungian psychology by Jungian analysts ; 140

BF109.J8G84 2014 150.19'54 C2013-907387-6

INNER CITY BOOKS
Box 1271, Station Q, Toronto, ON M4T 2P4, Canada.
Telephone 416) 927-0355. NO FAX.
Toll.free in Canada and U.S.: 1-888-927-0355
www.innercitybooks.net / booksales@innercitybooks.net

INNER CITY BOOKS was founded in 1980 to promote the understanding and practical application of the work of C. G. Jung.

Cover: "The Feminine Mystique," pen and ink, 2010, by Amanda Kirk.

Printed and bound in Canada by Thistle Printing Limited.

For Carlos, my friend, my soul mate, my master, my husband, my love.

CONTENTS

See final pages for other Inner City titles and how to order

ODE TO PHANES/EROS

Phanes is the God who rises agleam from the waters. / Phanes is the smile of dawn. / Phanes is the resplendent day. / He is the immortal present. / He is the gushing streams. / He is the soughing wind. / He is hunger and satiation. / He is love and lust. / He is mourning and consolation. / He is promise and fulfillment. / He is the light that illuminates every darkness. / He is the eternal day. / He is the silver light of the moon. / He is the flickering stars. / He is the shooting star that flashes and falls and lapses. / He is the stream of shooting stars that returns every year. / He is the returning sun and moon. / He is the trailing star that brings wars and noble wine. / He is the good and fullness of the year. / He fulfills the hours with life-filled enchantment. / He is love's embrace and whisper. / He is the warmth of friendship. / He is the hope that enlivens the void. / He is the magnificence of all renewed suns. / He is the joy at every birth. / He is the blooming flowers. / He is the velvety butterfly's wing. / He is the scent of blooming gardens that fills the nights. / He is the song of joy. / He is the tree of light. / He is perfection, everything done better. / He is everything euphonious. / He is the well-measured. / He is the sacred number. / He is the promise of life. / He is the contract and the sacred pledge. / He is the diversity of sounds and colors. / He is the sanctification of morning, noon, and evening. / He is the benevolent and the gentle. / He is salvation... / In truth, Phanes is the happy day... / In truth, Phanes is work and its accomplishment and its remuneration. / He is the troublesome task and the evening calm. / He is the step on the middle way; its beginning, its middle, and its end. / He is foresight. / He is the end of fear. / He is the sprouting seed, the opening bud. / He is the gate of reception, of acceptance and deposition. / He is the spring and the desert. / He is the safe haven and the stormy night. / He is the certainty in desperation. / He is the solid in dissolution. / He is the liberation from imprisonment. / He is counsel and strength in advancement. / He is the friend of man, the light emanating from man, the bright glow that man beholds on his path. / He is the greatness of man, his worth, and his force.

Philemon's description of Phanes/Eros,
September 11, 1917[1] *(See below, p. 81).*

FOREWORD

The *Red Book* was always a true legend in the Jungian movement. It was thought to reveal the great secrets of the master's life. Few people had seen it, but their description of it and the Jung family's resistance to publication of it, turned it into a true mystery. The fact that we knew that the original was in a bank safe in the center of Zurich, made it a coveted and irresistible treasure.

When the book was finally published in New York, in October 2009, Maria Helena and I felt that we could not absent ourselves from such an important event. After following and teaching Jung's theory for so many years, the call to be there came to us with great force.

Based on thirteen years of research, the historian Sonu Shamdasani solemnly started the lecture presenting the book he had edited. And, in front of hundreds of white-haired analysts, he declared with great assurance that all of us should begin to read Jung's work anew, because, arising from the *Red Book*, a new Jung would emerge.

From the beginning of its publication, two formal aspects were greatly emphasized. The first was the method of active imagination, in which Jung dialogues in his imagination with extraordinary psychic figures. The second was a series of distinct paintings and a text of exuberant fantasy, in highly elaborated calligraphy from medieval Germany compatible with a sacred text.

Since then, two additional matters were greatly commented. The first was Jung's fear, and the belief of various psychologists and psychoanalysts, that the book had been written within a delirious psychotic state which would explain many of his imaginings and fantasies. The principal "symptom" of this state was a vision or hallucination Jung had in 1913, in which the map of Europe was covered in blood. He was horrified and really thought he was schizophrenic.

The second was that he courageously pursued his imaginings, and in 1914, with the start of the First World War, he realized that he had not had an hallucination but rather a prospective psychic vision of what was about to happen and, for this reason, he was not schizophrenic, but gifted with great sensibility and intuition.

He and Shamdasani also greatly emphasized that the principal concepts of his work, such as the transcendent function, the archetypes of anima and Self, and the process of individuation were expressed in dreams and visions in the *Red Book*, which would configure the discovery of a new method of scientific research, utilizing dreams, fantasies, and active imagination.

The secret book that would reveal Jung's creative and perhaps psychotic life, in this way came especially to demonstrate his courage, his genius, and a new way to do science, which definitively marked him as the founder of modern psychology, alongside Freud.

Examining the contents of the book, I confirmed the creativity, the originality, and the courage that Jung displayed by writing it, but I did not find properly a thread that could link its content as a whole to an individual myth, to Jung's process of individuation, to existential details that really characterize life as it is.

It was in this context that I accompanied my wife, Maria Helena, in her serious study of the *Red Book*, and her discovery of an Ariadne's thread that suddenly became for me a clear account of an absolutely personal story line, the light and the shadow, charged with seeking, suffering, guilt, and self-realization that, now, we see corresponds to what Jung described later as the process of individuation.

Indeed, Jung's amours have been almost as much of a mystery as the *Red Book*. I hope the reader has the same pleasure that I had in following the Eros-thread from his wife Emma through his patient Sabina Spielrein to his long-time muse Tony Wolff, and so to the creation of the *Red Book* as uncovered by Maria Helena in this extraordinary account of how Jung came to develop the concepts of anima, Self and individuation.

Carlos Byington

Sao Paulo

INTRODUCTION

There is no more hypocritical whore than the intellect
when it replaces the heart[2].

What Is C. G. Jung's *Red Book?*

The *Red Book*, or *Liber Novus*, in which Swiss psychiatrist Carl Gustav Jung poured his imagination, his creativity and artistic endowment, was for many years a sort of fetish among Jungians. The fact of its existence and importance were already well known—Jung himself made this revelation, mentioning it in his memoirs and showing the book to a few people. But the enormous volume written in gothic calligraphic text, filled with illuminations and paintings, with a red leather cover justifying its name, was for many years kept in a safety deposit box in a bank in the heart of Zurich's financial center, far from the eyes of the Jungian community. Although it is known that many of Jung's written materials and recordings from his seminars have yet to be published, the *Red Book* has always held a special place for Jungians, because it was widely accepted that this book was an extraordinary work.

Jung writes in *Memories, Dreams, Reflections*:

> The years when I was pursuing my inner images were the most important in my life—in them everything essential was decided. It all began then; the later details are only supplements and clarifications of the material that burst forth from the unconscious, and at first swamped me. It was the *prima materia* for a lifetime's work[3].

He also relates, in his memoirs, some of his experiences during this time that encompasses his separation from Freud, the outbreak of the First World War, and what he called his "confrontation with the unconscious," wherein he believed he was threatened by schizophrenia.

All of these ingredients, revealed through minute glimpses, sharpened the imagination of his disciples. And when Sonu Shamdasani, a historian who received the Jung family's consent to publish the *Red Book*, made this announcement to those present at the XVI International Congress for

Analytical Psychology in 2004 in Barcelona, I felt a certain *frisson* in the audience. Soon the Jungian community would have its curiosity about the inner life of the master satisfied, and the great work would no longer be restricted to a few.

A book containing the fantasies, active imagination, paintings, as well as the foundation of Jung's thinking, for decades occupied the imagination of those studying analytical psychology. Shamdasani refers to this when he states, in the first page of his "Introduction" to the *Red Book*, that few unpublished works have exerted such an effect on the social and intellectual history of the twentieth century.

Today we are aware that Jung was divided over whether or not to publish the book. Nevertheless the presentation, the content often addressed to "my friends," and the epilogue added in 1959, demonstrate that he knew one day the book would become public. During his lifetime Jung disclosed parts of its contents here and there, such as some mandalas in *The Secret of the Golden Flower* (1929) and *Concerning Mandala Symbolism* (1950), and the "Seven Sermons to the Dead" in his book *Memories, Dreams, Reflections* (1961)[4]. We also find mention of some of these experiences in his seminars, such as *Seminar on Analytical Psychology* (1925), as well as the retelling of some of his dreams published in "Case Z" in *The Psychological Aspects of the Kore* (1941).

Nearly a century after its beginning, the *Red Book* came to light in its original form. The book launch, in October 2009, deeply moved the Jungian world. Its impressive presentation, the beauty of its images, the details of its calligraphic text, and the foreboded depth of its content caused admiration, surprise, amazement, reverence, respect and even feelings of religiosity. The first edition sold out quickly, as did the special limited edition of 199 highly priced copies.

Construction of the *Red Book*

In the editorial note on page 225 of the *Red Book*, Shamdasani mentions the dates of the manuscripts underlying *Liber Novus* (the name Jung gave to the *Red Book*), which is divided into *Liber Primus*, *Liber Secundus* and *Scrutinies*. The first two parts arise from the *Black Books* 2-5, dated

December 1913 to April 1914; the handwritten draft, written during the summer of 1914 to 1915; and the typed drafts (1915), corrected drafts (with corrections around 1915 and 1920) and other sources. The Caligraphic Volume, that is, the manuscript in gothic script, was made by Jung from 1915 to 1930, was taken up again in 1959, but was left incomplete. There are also the transcriptions by Cary Baynes (1924-1925), the Yale Manuscript, and a copy edited from the drafts of the *Liber Primus*. The *Scrutinies* originate from the *Black Books* 5 and 6, written between April 1914 and June 1916, and a calligraphic and a printed copy of the *Seven Sermons* (1916), the handwritten draft (around 1917), the typed draft (around 1918), and an incomplete transcription made by Cary Baynes (27 pages). We must be conscious of these dates, so that we can distinguish between those that refer to the emergence of the **content** of the experiences related in the *Red Book* and those associated mainly with its form and paintings.

From 1915 to 1930 Jung made some changes to the original text and included the paintings. But the central theme of the *Red Book* is based, above all, on what Jung experienced from October 1913 to June 1914—in spite of the fact that he interrupted the book when he was transcribing, in *Liber Secundus*, the experiences he went through in February 1914. As we have seen, Jung also did not write the *Scrutinies* into the *Red Book*. They were transcribed by Shamdasani from Jung's drafts, allowing us greater insight into the development of Jung's individuation process.

It was in 1915 that Jung began to transcribe his experiences into the *Liber Novus*, possibly with the intention of making the book public one day. In order to better grasp the meaning of the *Red Book*, we must keep in mind a few points that will help to contextualize the work and facilitate our comprehension of Jung's development process:

In beginning the first chapter, *Liber Primus*, Jung is transcribing, in 1915, from the *Black Books* what he experienced in 1913 and 1914.

Shamdasani transcribed three Appendices at the end of the *Red Book*. The second (Appendix B, p. 365) provides Jung's commentary on some of the images presented in the *Red Book* and was copied from the corrected draft written between 1915 and 1920.

JUNG AND THE SEARCH FOR INTEGRATION OF LOVE

The color red points to Eros[5].

Experiences

The *Red Book* contains such abundant material that Jung admits having spent the rest of his life elaborating it. The experiences described in the *Red Book* originated many theoretical concepts, which Jung developed throughout his work. However, which life experiences contributed to the emergence of the content Jung carefully started to document in 1913?

Jung seems to offer a glimpse of the element that launched these experiences when, in 1914, he writes that sadness accompanied him until June 24 of that year, when his soul spoke to him ("The greatest comes to the smallest,") and then kept silent. Soon, the First World War broke out and that, together with consciousness of all he had lived, gave him courage to reveal what is written in the *Red Book*. During the following year the voices from the depths remained silent[6].

Designating the war the triggering element of his experience, Jung induced his readers to think so. Shamdasani[7], mentioning Jung's lecture on *The Psychological Foundations of Belief in Spirits* given in 1919, declares that Jung distinguished two situations in which the collective unconscious becomes active. The first is when there is a crisis in the life of the individual, and the second is in times of great political, social, or religious turmoil. According to Jung, intuitive people sense what is to come, anticipating the still subliminal collective unrest. These individuals try to express to the community what they foresee. By virtue of the impersonal character of this sort of experience, Jung considered it arising from the collective unconscious. This is how shamans function. They have "great dreams" that bring useful messages for the tribe.

Therefore, according to Shamdasani, following Jungian theory, material arising from Jung's subjective experience was interpreted as belonging to the collective unconscious and awakened as a result of great general cultural unrest[8].

Further along, Shamdasani[9] insists on this idea, declaring that Jung's visions about the war were prophetic, premonitory, and led him to produce the *Red Book*, or *Liber Novus*.

Jung also associates the period of his rupture from Freud to the time he developed the technique of active imagination, which he considered of immense importance to elaborate symbolically difficult situations. He said that this technique makes sense when one is under the impression that there is no way out, adding that he felt this way when he separated from Freud[10].

On the other hand, Aniela Jaffé, to whom Jung related his memoirs, wrote to the Bollingen Foundation in 1957 informing them that Jung had suggested that the *Liber Novus* and the *Black Books* be donated to the library of the University of Basel but should remain restricted for 50 years, 80 years, or more, since "he hates the idea that anybody should read this material without knowing the relations to his life"[11]. A few years earlier, around 1952, with Jung's support, Cary Baynes was thinking of writing a biography of Jung based on *Liber Novus*[12].

At eighty-two years of age, Jung felt it was important that the reader of this material know its connections to his life; that the content of his imagination should be related to his existential experiences. Contrary to what he proposed in *The Visions Seminars*, conducted between 1930 and 1934 and published in 1976, when he stated that he would deliberately omit the personal events of the life of the patient, whose case he was going to expose, since "we are all spellbound by those circumstances and they distract our minds from the real thing, which is that we ourselves are split inside"[13], Jung now stressed the importance of personal data. In fact, even the more collective and overall experiences are rooted in the life endured by the individual, in his/her personality, and always need something or someone to express them.

So much so that if a patient relates a particular dream we always ask for his or her personal associations, no matter how much its images can be acknowledged as universal. This is because the meaning of a dream is attached, always and invariably, to an individual context.

It is beyond a doubt that the *Red Book* was written during the time that

Jung split from Freud. It's also true that its content emerged in the period prior to the First World War. But another no less important event occurred in Jung's life at the end of 1912, when he decided to carry on his love relationship with Toni Wolff.

In my view, when we read the *Red Book* in light of the relationship between Jung and Wolff, we can understand many things that otherwise remain obscure. The connection between the material published in the *Red Book* and biographical data on Jung, obtained mainly through the books of Barbara Hannah[14] and Deirdre Bair[15], and also contained in the *Red Book*'s "Introduction," written by Sonu Shamdasani—historian, editor, and one of the translators of this work to English—give validity to this argument.

The proposal of my book is to show that the dramatic love relationship between Jung and Wolff is the conductive thread throughout the *Red Book*. Love and its emotions will lead us to understand Jung's process of individuation as described in the *Red Book*.

To follow this path, I think it is important to present some data from Jung's life in the period that precedes the onset of his amorous relationship with Toni Wolff.

1910

In 1910, twenty-two years old and depressed because of the death of her father, Toni Wolff was referred to Jung.

Born into a wealthy family on September 18, 1888, she was the eldest of three sisters. Her father did not permit his girls to pursue a formal education because he felt it could become an impediment when the time came to find a husband. However, he authorized the girls to attend informal classes, even at universities. Wolff was always drawn to the study of religion, theology, philosophy, and mythology. Highly intelligent, erudite, and having similar interests as Jung, it is not hard to imagine the attraction this young girl awakened in him.

Wolff is thought to be someone—perhaps the only such person—who could talk with Jung as an equal, discussing his ideas and contributing to them with her own point of view:

> [...] and often hers presented strikingly different interpretations from what he first envisioned. From the beginning, she contributed an independent perspective to his work, and her part of their conversation was peppered more frequently with remarks such as "yes, but..." than with the simple "yes."[16]

Hannah[17] describes Wolff as the most appropriate person she met to carry the projection of the anima, meaning a type of woman who can easily correspond to what a man is fond of. Thus, due to the characteristics of Wolff's personality, there is a strong probability that one can apply to her relationship with Jung what he says about the encounter between man and his anima:

> A man may [...] know the real woman also as lightness and darkness, but when he sees in a woman the magical quality that is the essence of She [of his anima], he at once begins tremendous projections of the unconscious upon her[18].

1911-1912

The closeness that developed between Jung and Freud during the years in which they worked together also occurred between their families. In the correspondence between Jung and Freud, letters from Emma Jung[19] to Freud were published in which she reveals some conjugal difficulty.

Worried that Freud might have an unfavorable reaction to Jung's book *Transformation and Symbols of the Libido* (published in the Collected Works as *Symbols of Transformation),* Emma writes a few letters to him. In one of them, dated 6 November 1911, Emma thanks Freud for his kind letter, and adds:

> The second reason [to write this letter] was provided by the conversation on the first morning after your arrival, when you told me about your family. You said then that your marriage had long been "amortized," now there was nothing more to do except—die. And the children were growing up and then they become a real worry, and yet this is the only true joy. This made such an impression on me and seemed to me so significant that I had to think of it again and again, and I fancied it was intended just for me because it was meant symbolically at the same time and referred to my husband.

> [...] I have found with Carl also that the imperative 'earn money' is only an evasion of something else to which he has resistances.[20]

In a letter to Freud dated 14 November of the same year, Emma signs off saying: "Please write nothing of this to Carl; things are going badly enough with me as it is"[21]. In a third letter to Freud, dated 24 November 1911, Emma opens up even more:

> [...] Please don't worry, I am not always as despondent as I was in my last letter [...] Usually I am quite at one with my fate and see very well how lucky I am, but from time to time I am tormented by the conflict about how I can hold my own against Carl. I find I have no friends, all the people who associate with us really only want to see Carl, except for a few boring and to me quite uninteresting persons.
>
> Naturally the women are all in love with him, and with the men I am instantly cordoned off as the wife of the father or friend. Yet I have a strong need for people and Carl too says I should stop concentrating on him and the children, but what on earth am I to do? What with my strong tendency to autoerotism it is very difficult, but also objectively it is difficult because I can never compete with Carl. In order to emphasize this I usually have to talk extra stupidly when in company.
>
> I do my best to get transferences and if they don't turn out as I wished I am always very depressed. You will now understand why I felt so bad at the thought that I had lost your favour, and I was also afraid Carl might notice something. At any rate he now knows about the exchange of letters, as he was astonished to see one of your letters addressed to me; [...][22].

Emma's letters are indicative that all was not going well in her relationship with her husband. It's not difficult to empathize with the suffering brought on by the presence of other women in Jung's life, especially knowing as we do today that his relationship with Wolff lasted until the end of her life (Wolff died in March 1953).

For a man of Jung's sensibility and depth, recently emerged from a tumultuous relationship with Sabina Spielrein, the conflict between collective moral values and the call of his own soul was an enormous drama, which required Herculean strength, as we see throughout the *Red*

Book. In 1912, Jung had an impressive dream, which he thought referred to his future rupture with Freud, although relations between the two remained satisfactory until the end of 1911, and Freud was initially positive in his reactions to *Transformation and Symbols of the Libido*, as can be inferred from the letter below, dated 12 November 1911:

> [...] One of the nicest works I have read (again), is that of a well known author on the 'Transformation and Symbols of the Libido'. In it many things are so well expressed that they seem to have taken on definitive form and in this form impress themselves on the memory. [...] it is the best thing this promising author has written, up to now [...].
>
> [...]
> Not least, I am delighted by the many points of agreement with things I have already said or would *like* to say. [...][23].

Here is the dream and the commentaries Jung relates in his memoirs:

> [The dream] had its scene in a mountainous region on the Swiss-Austrian border. It was toward evening, and I saw an elderly man in the uniform of an Imperial Austrian customs official. He walked past, somewhat stooped, without paying any attention to me. His expression was peevish, rather melancholic and vexed. There were others present, and someone informed me that the old man was not really there, but was the ghost of a customs official who had died years ago. "He is one of those who still couldn't die properly." That was the first part of the dream.
>
> [...]
> [...] after a hiatus came a second and far more remarkable part. I was in an Italian city, and it was around noon, between twelve and one o'clock. A fierce sun was beating down upon the narrow streets. The city was built on hills and reminded me of a particular part of Basel, the Kohlenberge. The little streets which lead down into the valley, the Birsigtal, that runs through the city, are partly flights of steps. In the dream, one such stairway descended to Barfüsserplatz. The city was Basel, and yet it was also an Italian city, something like Bergamo. It was summertime; the blazing sun stood at the zenith, and everything was bathed in an intense light. A crowd came streaming toward me, and I knew that the shops were closing and people were on their way home to dinner. In the midst of this stream of people walked a knight in full armor. He mounted the steps toward me. He

wore a helmet of the kind that is called a basinet, with eye slits, and chain armor. Over this was a white tunic which was woven, front and back, a large red cross.

One can easily imagine how I felt: suddenly to see in a modern city, during the noonday rush hour, a crusader coming toward me. What struck me as particularly odd was that none of the many persons walking about seemed to notice him. No one turned his head or gazed after him. It was as though he were completely invisible to everyone but me. I asked myself what this apparition meant, and then it was as if someone answered me—but there was no one there to speak: "Yes, this is a regular apparition. The knight always passes by here between twelve and one o'clock, and has been doing so for a very long time [for centuries, I gathered] and everyone knows about it"[24].

Jung interprets the first half of the dream as relating to Freud, considering the borders that existed between their opinions, and the dream itself as compensation for his attitude of esteem and admiration[25]. He also states that during this time he was "oppressed and bewildered"[26]. As for the second part of the dream, he sets the customs official and the knight in opposition, since while the first "couldn't die properly," the knight "was full of life and completely real"[27].

In spite of the interpretation Jung himself gives to his dream, and considering that the interpretation of one's own dreams is a difficult enough task, I suggest we compare the two halves of the dream. In the first, it is almost night; the setting, the Swiss-Austrian border; the character, a customs officer. In the second half, the sun is at its peak; the scene unfolds in Italy; character in focus, a knight (a crusader).

Placing these oneiric elements side by side, we see that the first half of the dream seems to refer to something that is being overcome: it's almost night, day is coming to an end, a cycle is closing. The Swiss-Austrian border, beyond the obvious association that it is the border formed by Freud and Jung's countries of origin, does not merely separate but is also a junction of these two countries, united by their Germanic roots and traditions (at least the part of Switzerland where Jung was born and lived). In addition, the customs officer is a public official, attached to a bureaucratic job and, so to speak, hardly heroic, creative, or challenging.

This part of the dream could be summed up in the dynamic of the employee, "who still couldn't die properly," who is overcome, but who still insists in occupying a space in life. He doesn't die but remains fixated, doesn't transform, but indefinitely repeats his dynamic, his functioning.

On the other hand, the second half of the dream seems to point to the future—a prospective aspect that indicates a vision of greater clarity in an Italian city. Contrary to the Swiss-Austrian psychology, rooted in Germanic culture, Italy has a Latin tradition that is warmer, more emotive, and even impassioned. The dynamism of the matriarchal archetype, linked among other things to sensuality, spontaneity, and intimacy[28], becomes much more explicit in Italian society than in its Swiss-Austrian counterpart. The knight, a crusader, is an itinerant man with a religious ideal and, as we will subsequently see, he is often amorous, and can be regarded as a representation of great dynamism, idealism, and vitality. It is as if the beginning of the dream points to what is fixed, bureaucratically repeating, say, without profound meaning in life. The second part, however, shows the possibility of a world full of life, actions, emotions.

Jung could only interpret the figure of the knight much later. In associating the dream image with his future interests, he said, "the knight belonged to the twelfth century. That was the time when alchemy was beginning and also the quest for the Holy Grail"[29].

The adventures of the knights of King Arthur's court emerged around the theme of the Grail. Among the knights, Lancelot deserves special attention for being the one in love with Guinevere, Arthur's wife. In the figure of Lancelot, love, adultery, and knighthood come together.

The twelfth century is characterized by the emergence of troubadours and romantic songs, courtly love, and service to "subtle love" (the *Minnedienst*). The troubadours, like wandering knights, were also itinerants.

According to Barros,

> Courtly Love can be seen as a new moment in the complex human history of ways of feeling and its forms of expression. Its emergence through troubadouresque poetry left so indelible marks on the Western repertory of aesthetic possibilities for the expression and experience of love, and in the Western males' imagination concerning the amorous subject, that **fre-**

quently the dawn of medieval troubadours in the twelfth century is pointed as the very instant of invention of romantic love in the West[30]. [emphasis mine.]

Among courtly love's characteristics a few deserve description, since they permit an analogy with Jung's individuation process, in which he sought to elaborate the principle of Eros and his feeling function, as can be surmised from this passage:

> Therefore Salome turns to me, because Eros is in need of help, and because I have apparently been enabled to behold this image for precisely this reason.[31]

Barros describes some attributes of courtly love:

> At the heart of all [is the figure of] an "Amateur" who gives himself over body and soul to an uncontrollable passion and to the dedicated loving service of his beloved woman. And she: a "Lady" who [...] is generally unattainable—or, for being spatially inaccessible (maybe because she lives in a far away country) or, who knows in this case maybe an even more insurmountable obstacle, for being *socially* inaccessible [...]
>
> Involving everything, a Love so extreme as ambiguous, bringing at once in the same movement an undisguised component of eroticization and an idealized dimension [...][32]

Courtly love contains aspects that are anti-matrimonial, since marriage might be an accommodation to social and familial interests and at times may occur without love. "Lovers give all, reciprocally and freely, without any obligation of necessity, while spouses are obliged, dutifully, to accept the desires of one another"[33].

It is important that courtly love is kept secret:

> The *metron*, virtue that makes the Amateur capable of behaving with temperance and moderation [...] must be cultivated and learned by the courtly lover, who realizes through love the betterment of his own spirit[34].

In Jungian terms, we can think about the search for love as part of the process of individuation, since it refers to the elaboration of the anima, in the case of men, and of the animus, its corresponding element in women. Jung's process was to seek his self-development through love, even keeping it partially secret and trying to adapt it to his marriage.

"To die for love," a notion coming from courtly poetry, "approximates courtly love of other systems of self surrender, such as Mystic Love, which ultimately aspires to merging with the Creator [...]"[35].

> All of these elements inhabit the plane of sensibility and—maybe for the first time with such intensity—threaten to bring feeling to an outstanding place in the medieval scene, even above religious faith, scholarly reason, daily utilitarianism[36].

Rewritten with a foundation in Jungian typology, the above paragraph expresses that when it is brought forth with the thundering intensity proposed by courtly love, the feeling function differs from religious faith, associated with the intuitive function; from scholarly reason, i.e., the thinking function; and daily utilitarianism, that is, the sensation function. So it was in the twelfth century, through courtly love, that the feeling function received great prominence and permitted a living experience of the dialectic, since this love "delights but makes one suffer, enhances but makes fragile, eroticizes but idealizes, educates but makes one mad, submits but ennobles"[37]. However, are not all these manifestations of the soul present in the *Red Book*?

Still in 1912, Jung related the following dream:

> Then, around Christmas of 1912, I had a dream. In the dream I found myself in a magnificent Italian loggia with pillars, a marble floor, and a marble balustrade. I was sitting on a gold Renaissance chair; in front of me was a table of rare beauty. It was made of green stone, like emerald. There I sat, looking out into the distance, for the loggia was set high up on the tower of a castle. My children were sitting at the table too.
>
> Suddenly a white bird descended, a small sea gull or a dove. Gracefully, it came to rest on the table, and I signed to the children to be still so that they would not frighten away the pretty white bird. Immediately, the dove was transformed into a little girl, about eight years of age, with golden blond hair. She ran off with the children and played with them among the colonnades of the castle.
>
> I remained lost in thought, musing about what I had just experienced.

The little girl returned and tenderly placed her arms around my neck. Then she suddenly vanished; the dove was back and spoke in a human voice. "Only in the first hours of the night can I transform myself into a human being, while the male dove is busy with the twelve dead." Then she flew off into the blue air, and I awoke[38].

In *The Psychological Aspects of the Kore*, Jung cites part of this dream as an example of manifestations of the anima as animal. This dream "shows the anima as elflike, i.e., only partially human. She can just as well be a bird, which means that she may belong wholly to nature and can vanish (i.e., become unconscious) from the human sphere (i.e., consciousness)"[39].

The dove transforms into a girl of approximately eight years of age. If we apply the same rationale that Jung uses in *The Psychology of the Transference*[40], we can consider that this was her age in 1912, while what she represents originally emerged in 1904: likely the same year that Jung began to see the winsome Sabina Spielrein[41].

Jung met Spielrein when she was confined at Burghölzli[42], during a psychotic break, or psychotic hysteria as Jung diagnosed it[43]. Jung treated her and they developed a tumultuous love affair. In his book, *A Secret Symmetry*, Carotenuto affirms that Spielrein could have represented a typical anima figure to Jung, "attracting and repelling, wondrous and diabolical, exciting and depressing"[44].

> [Jung] let himself go completely, and this unhappy woman, obsessed by disgust and the notion of the feces that everywhere surrounded her, became a graceful feminine image who, in a boat on the Lake of Zurich, revealed to Jung the world of feeling and of overwhelming love, free of that bourgeois hypocrisy that forces the man and woman to live an everlasting and humiliating lie. Sabina would seem to have been a woman for whom love did not imply calculation or the demand for promises that are broken the moment they are made, a Dionysiac woman, vibrant with feeling, who understood and forgave everything while offering Jung a forceful spur for his spiritual growth.[45]

The important place Jung gave love in his life became naturally veiled and obfuscated by his immense creativity and his work. However, in the letters that he wrote to Spielrein he demonstrates dissatisfaction with his marriage, and exposes his vital and vigorous nature that desired love and sought it out.

> You cannot imagine how much it means to me to have hopes of loving a person whom I must not condemn, and who does not condemn herself, to being smothered in the banality of habit. (Letter from Jung to Spielrein, June 30, 1908)[46]
>
> I am looking for a person who can love without punishing, imprisoning and draining the other person; I am seeking this as yet unrealized type who will manage to separate love from social advantage or disadvantage, so that love may always be an end unto itself, not just a means for achieving another end.
>
> [...]
>
> It is my misfortune that my life means nothing to me without the joy of love, of tempestuous, eternally changing love. (Letter from Jung to Spielrein, December 4, 1908)[47]

Although they maintained a professional correspondence until 1918, Jung begins to distance himself emotionally from Spielrein in 1909. On March 7, 1909, Jung writes to Freud:

> [...] Meanwhile I have learned an unspeakable amount of marital wisdom, for until now I had a totally inadequate idea of my polygamous components despite all self-analysis. Now I know where and how the devil can be laid by the heels. These painful yet extremely salutary insights have churned me up hellishly inside, but for that very reason, I hope, have secured the moral qualities which will be of the greatest advantage to me in later life. The relationship with my wife has gained enormously in assurance and depth … I think I have now entered the stage of convalescence, thanks to the buffetings fate has given me.[48]

When, in 1912, Jung has the above-described dream, he writes in his *Black Book* 2 that this dream was responsible for his decision to enter into an amorous relationship with Toni Wolff[49].

Thus, four years after declaring his need for love to Sabina, Jung admits again to be living a great love. Trying to remain faithful to his nature, willing to follow its calling, incapable or not wishing to deny its manifestation, Jung becomes involved with Toni Wolff and has a love relationship with her lasting forty-three years, until her death in 1953.

In exposing experiences of his relationship with Spielrein to Freud (see his letter from March 1909) Jung states, "these painful yet extremely salutary insights have churned me up hellishly inside." In considering his relationship to Wolff, it is not difficult to imagine a similar intensity of inner conflict. He fell in love, but he was married and had children, in a society where the expectation was to uphold marriage. Additionally, in 1912 he was insecure about Freud's reactions to his book *Transformation and Symbols of the Libido.* Mobilization typical of passion, added to his geniality, creativity, sensibility, intelligence, interest in the psychic life, guilt, despair, anguish, and suffering, constellated intense and profound experiences in Jung, a type of avalanche of symbols that clamored for expression. This material is presented in the *Red Book,* a work that Toni Wolff did not want to see published. Cary Baynes—a contemporary of Jung who translated a few pages to English—wished to have it published and could not understand why Wolff did not[50].

In 1915, when Jung began to transcribe the *Red Book*, he remembered that Wolff had sunk into a process similar to the one that involved him. He thought, on that occasion, he could discuss some of his experiences with her, but she was just as confused and disoriented, and like him, "was experiencing a similar stream of images"[51]. He added that his wife was unable to help him with this[52]. Years later, in *Memories, Dreams, Reflections*, Jung states that he no longer carried on such conversations with his anima, "for I no longer have such emotions"[53], demonstrating that emotions are the *prima materia* of this kind of experience.

The very language Jung uses in the *Red Book* is not of one in his or her usual state of mind, but rather the expression of someone in love, of a poet, in whose consciousness transformed by love metaphors flourish.

I therefore consider the essence of the *Red Book* to be the result of Jung's simultaneous relationship with Toni Wolff and Emma Jung, and of the feelings and emotions arising from it. My aim is to bring to light this essence by studying in detail the content of Jung's formidable book.

LIBER PRIMUS

Love, soul, and God are beautiful and terrible[54].

The Spirit of This Time and the Spirit of the Depths

Jung begins the *Red Book* with a chapter titled "The Way of What is to Come." In it, he describes what he calls the "spirit of this time" and the "spirit of the depths." It is worth noting that his descriptions are full of emotion. Throughout the *Red Book*, Jung powerfully expresses his experience, his conflict, and often his resistance to submitting to what impels him from within—"I have no choice, but I must"[55]. Jung's language is metaphoric, dense, vibrant, and in many instances—why not say—epic.

From the beginning of the book, Jung reveals the great antagonism existing between the constituent poles of these two spirits. Identifying with the "spirit of this time," which is linked to utility, valor, and collective values, he had tried to keep the "spirit of the depths" at a distance[56], unaware that the latter had greater strength than the former. However, he admits:

> [the spirit of this time] let devotion to the ideals of this time die out in me. He forced me down to the last and simplest things.
>
> The spirit of the depths took my understanding and all my knowledge and placed them at the service of the inexplicable and the paradoxical. He robbed me of speech and writing for everything that was not in his service, namely the melting together of sense and nonsense, which produces the supreme meaning.[57]

He adds: "But the supreme meaning is the path, the way and the bridge to what is to come"[58].

Thus, the ultimate meaning, the fruit of the spirit of the depths, is the path that would take him to God. Like an initial dream in analysis that brings a prognosis, the beginning of the *Red Book* shows that Jung's process will lead him to an image of God through the spirit of the depths.

But what other attributes belong to the spirit of the depths? It subjugates Jung's arrogance of desire to bring recognition only to the greatness of the ultimate meaning, was in line with the spirit of this time.

> I had to swallow the small as a means of healing the immortal in me. It completely burnt up my innards since it was inglorious and unheroic. It was even ridiculous and revolting. But the pliers of the spirit of the depths held me, and I had to drink the bitterest of all draughts.
>
> [...]
>
> I resisted recognizing that the everyday belongs to the image of the Godhead. I fled this thought, I hid myself behind the highest and coldest stars. But the spirit of the depths caught up with me, and forced the bitter drink between my lips.[59]

In the pages that follow, Jung vividly describes the conflict between both spirits. Although he tried to align himself with the spirit of this time, the spirit of the depths always had the last word, leading him, despite his resistance, to do what he felt he *must* do. By way of example, I transcribe here an excerpt from one of the clashes between the two spirits:

> But the spirit of the depths spoke to me and said: "To understand a thing is a bridge and possibility of returning to the path. But to explain a matter is arbitrary and sometimes even murder. Have you counted the murderer among the scholars?"
>
> But the spirit of this time stepped up to me and laid before me huge volumes which contained all my knowledge. Their pages were made of ore, and a steel stylus had engraved inexorable words in them, and he pointed to these inexorable words and spoke to me, and said: "What you speak, that is madness."
>
> It is true, it is true, what I speak is the greatness and intoxication and ugliness of madness.
>
> But the spirit of the depths stepped up to me and said: "What you speak is. The greatness is, the intoxication is, the undignified, sick, paltry dayliness is. It runs in all the streets, lives in all the houses, and rules the day of all humanity. Even the eternal stars are commonplace. It is the great mistress and the one essence of God. One laughs about it, and laughter, too, is. Do you believe, man of this time, that laughter is lower than worship? Where is your measure, false measurer? The sum of life decides in laughter and in worship, not your judgment."[60]

The tension unravels between these two points of view, between explanation and knowledge, worship and laughter. And Jung feels that what he says is madness.

In fact, we see that the spirit of this time associates itself to convention, tradition, adaptation to the collective, while the spirit of the depths points to originality, innovation, spontaneity, and transgression for the sake of the individual. The first is more formal, rational, and logical; the second, its opposite, brings the logic of the heart, of images, and of metaphors.

That is the context in which Jung introduces his experiences. Anguish and tension reveal themselves in expressions associated with the body—he had to swallow the small one, drink the most bitter of drinks; his entrails were destroyed by fire. In the *Red Book*, Jung relates:

> One of the greatest difficulties for me lay in dealing with my negative feelings. I was voluntarily submitting myself to emotions of which I could not really approve [...] It cost me a great deal to undergo them, but I had been challenged by fate. [...]
>
> In order to grasp the fantasies which were stirring in me "underground," I knew that I had to let myself plummet down into them, as it were. I felt not only violent resistance to this, but a distinct fear. For I was afraid of losing command of myself and becoming a prey to the fantasies—and as a psychiatrist I realized only too well what that meant.[61]

This mobilization of energy, nevertheless, could only happen if there were an intense enough trigger element, something in his life that were as proportionally strong as the torrent of content that affected him.

Bloodied Europe

One experience that profoundly marked Jung occurred in October 1913. He describes it in the *Red Book* and repeats his story in *Memories, Dreams, Reflection:*

> I saw a monstrous flood covering all the northern and low-lying lands between the North Sea and the Alps. When it came up to Switzerland I saw that the mountains grew higher to protect our country. I realized that a frightful catastrophe was in progress. I saw the mighty yellow waves, the floating rubble of civilization, and the drowned bodies of uncounted thousands. Then the whole sea turned to blood. This vision lasted about one

hour. I was perplexed and nauseated, and ashamed of my weakness.

Two weeks passed; then the vision recurred, under the same conditions, even more vividly than before, and the blood was more emphasized. An inner voice spoke. "Look at it well; it is wholly real and it will be so. You cannot doubt it."[62]

It had not occurred to Jung to consider the possibility of war. Actually, he believed he was under the threat of psychosis[63]. We know that in a little more than a year and a half, the First World War would erupt. Jung felt relief in being able to associate war with his visions and perceive them, thus, as fruit of his intuition, of his capacity to foresee, and also as carriers of a more collective rather than individual dimension.

In the personal arena, however, the first time this vision occurred he was traveling alone. According to Bair[64], he was on his way to Schaffhausen to pick up his family who had been on an extended vacation at Emma's mother's house. As we've seen, Jung had decided to have a love relationship with Toni Wolff at the end of 1912, after a dream in which a dove transforms into a little girl (described above on pages 23-24).

[Jung] equated any knowledge and insight gained at this time (around 1912) with "[falling] in love with women" and "say[ing] yes to it. He said it was the time when the "anima" was first manifested, but he did not yet understand its significance.[65]

In 1925 while presenting a series of seminars, Jung recounted this vision and the dream I referred to before. Esther Harding, an American Jungian analyst who was in the audience, asked him to discuss the personal aspects of his fantasies a little more, to which Jung responded:

I could be taken as Switzerland fenced in by mountains, and the submergence of the world could be the debris of my former relationships.

You remember when I tried to describe the condition surrounding the fantasy I spoke of the […] feeling I had had of the thing being atmospheric.[66]

In 1913, the year coinciding with his rupture from Freud, Jung was absent from Küsnacht for five weeks while traveling to the United States; he spent a month in military service; he went to London and various German cities, and took holidays in the Swiss Alps and the North of Italy[67]. In June of this same year, Emma became pregnant for the fifth time.

In October, as Jung was picking up the family and bringing them home, consumed by his extra conjugal relationship and dealing with professional difficulties, we can think that the image of a catastrophe hitting Europe, beyond its prospective collective character, also reflected on an individual level the enormous tension he was experiencing.

Jung belonged to bourgeois society during a time in which separation was frowned upon. Two years earlier, Oskar Pfister, a protestant minister belonging to the psychoanalytic group, played a most prominent role in a scandal in Swiss society when he wanted to divorce because he had fallen in love with his cousin. He even was threatened to have his parish taken from him. He retreated having resolved "not to stand apart from the prevailing moral standards of the community"[68]. Marriage to Emma assured Jung of status and social stability, and also financial security, since she and her sister were inheritors of the second largest fortune in Switzerland. And Jung already feared for his professional life due to his separation from Freud[69].

Jung was frightened by the vision of a devastated Europe, which appeared to him as a sign of a possible schizophrenia. He didn't notice, at this moment, that this possible schizophrenia might symbolize his inner division: being in love with one woman and married to another. When the war broke out, Jung felt relief and gave himself permission to relate his experiences, since he had projected his internal conflict onto a war of global proportions. Thus, what happened externally gave Jung relief from guilt, and the liberty and tranquility that allowed him to share his experiences.

It is significant to note that Wolff was the only person to read the *Black Books* at the beginning of 1914[70]. Deirdre Bair states: "reading between the lines in documentary evidence, I surmise that he [Jung] permitted Emma to read portions of it [of the *Black Books*] in early 1915"[71]. Thus, only after the breakout of the war had given him an opportunity to project his experiences onto it and masked the marital crisis motivated by an overwhelming passion, did Jung allow his wife to read this material.

On the one hand, he had the necessity to be faithful to his experience, his emotions and feelings. On the other, he had the desire to remain in line with society, to maintain his persona, to recognize himself as he had always been, valorizing reason, coherence, science, and believing he could control his soul. This was the great tension, the power play between the spirit of the depths and the spirit of this time.

Jung could not resist his internal calling, because he felt that within each of us is the call for self-realization, "the way, the truth, and the life."[72]. Here he expresses what he will later conceive as individuation, the process that impels people to fulfill their essential nature, the development of consciousness. According to Jung, this process would begin in the second half of life, sparked by a moral crisis[73].

Jung writes that in 1913, when he had the vision of the flood, that is, of a bloodied Europe, it occurred at a very significant time for him. At midlife, he had achieved everything that he desired: power, wealth, fame, knowledge. But, it is exactly in this phase that the things one most covets no longer make so much sense, and one begins to seek something more essential that gives meaning to life. This crisis is accompanied by great impact and, in Jung's case, even horror[74].

In 1913, Jung attributed his vision of bloodied Europe to the spirit of the depths, and in November, a month afterwards, he began to write, calling forth his soul. We see, therefore, that this vision—or better, the spirit of the depths—awakened a yearning for the soul, which Jung would later call anima.

In Search of the Soul

Jung conceived the archetype of the anima as the image of the feminine in the psyche of man. The archetype of the anima in man and of the animus in woman mobilize a search for the Other with whom one can establish a symmetrical relationship, in which there does not exist—or at least should not exist—any hierarchy, as with friends, boyfriend and girlfriend, lovers, spouses. Anima and animus are always activated when one falls in love.

In Jung's case, the archetype of the anima comes through his beloved woman, Toni Wolff, who activates his unconscious and results in the eruption of the contents of the *Red Book*.

My soul, where are you? Do you hear me? I speak, I call you—are you there? I have returned, I am here again. I have shaken the dust of all the lands from my feet, and I have come to you, I am with you. After long years of long wandering, I have come to you again. Should I tell you everything I have seen, experienced, and drunk in? Or do you not want to hear about all the noise of life and the world? But one thing you must know: the one thing I have learned is that one must live this life.

This life is the way, the long sought-after way to the unfathomable, which we call divine. There is no other way, all other ways are false paths. I found the right way, it led me to you, to my soul. I return, tempered and purified. Do you still know me? How long the separation lasted! Everything has become so different. And how did I find you? How strange my journey was! What words should I use to tell you on what twisted paths a good star has guided me to you? Give me your hand, my almost forgotten soul. How warm the joy at seeing you again, you long disavowed soul. Life has led me back to you. Let us thank the life I have lived for all the happy and all the sad hours, for every joy, for every sadness. My soul, my journey should continue with you. I will wander with you and ascend to my solitude.[75]

The beginning of this speech has an uncanny resemblance to the clamor of Saint John of the Cross' *Spiritual Canticle*, a poem belonging to the book *Dark Night of the Soul*. In it, the soul searches for his Bridegroom, who left her. The Bridegroom, a metaphor for God, is not only the beloved, the longed for, the desired, but also the one who hurt her by departing. In the poetry of Saint John of the Cross the soul in love seeking her love object is the mystic expression of the soul seeking transcendence, union with the ultimate reality, an experience of totality through love. In his search for the soul—as we now know, through love—Jung yearned to find her and also his most profound essence, that which he would years later call Self.

The tension between the spirit of the depths and the spirit of this time, however, persisted because although Jung's values were more in line with the latter, the former ended up overpowering him, impeding his resistance through its strength.

He affirms that he had thought a lot and spoken quite a bit about the soul. He knew how to refer to her with scholarly words, judging and evaluating her with the perspective of a scientist. He transformed the soul into an object of study, believed her possible to be encompassed and dissected. But then he realized that it wasn't like that. The soul might seem subjugated, but judgment and knowledge belong to her, because she encompasses them. Thanks to the spirit of the depths, Jung was forced to speak with his soul, to call upon his soul. And in seeking her, he discovered that he had lost her[76]. This reminds us of Jung's statement that for eleven years he had been wandering and distant from his soul, and that he stopped writing in his diary in 1902—he married Emma in 1903[77].

The spirit of the depths led Jung to discover the autonomy of the anima, of the soul, and the impossibility of subjugating her to the will of the ego. She could not be circumscribed by reason, nor reduced to a scientific object, as she is much broader than the rational mind. The spirit of the depths taught him to see the soul as a living being, with its own existence, and he withdrew from her the perspective of the spirit of this time —with which he had identified—for whom the soul could be judged and encompassed by reason[78].

Being in love favors the projection mechanism by which we see in the Other something belonging to our own personality, but which we don't yet recognize as such. The more unconscious we are about a given characteristic or condition, the more intense the projection. The withdrawal of projections is, therefore, an important step towards the path to self-knowledge. And this is precisely what Jung perceives and writes about when he refers to the importance of creating a space between the person (or object) that constellates the anima, and the anima itself, since the soul is not found in objects of desire, but in the desire itself. This awareness permits the differentiation, for example, between the beloved woman and the image that she calls forth in man.

The possibility of differentiating between the desire in itself and the object of desire is what permits us to recognize that desire belongs to the soul itself, while the object, seen as Other, is experienced as separate from the subject. This process allows the removal of projections and the integration in the individual's personality of the content activated by them. Recognition of this distinction is crucial to a person in a state of intense projection of anima or animus, such as when falling in love, so that he or she may avoid fomenting an exaggeratedly symbiotic and indiscriminate relationship.

Jung also observed the importance of adequately feeding the soul, since the contrary leads to her transformation into a devouring beast. If a psychic content needs to be brought to consciousness to attain a greater equilibrium in the personality, its avoidance is equivalent to feeding the enemy. When certain experiences are very hard to be contained by the ego, when a person cannot deal with an emotion, the person might repress, negate, or use any other defense mechanism to keep it away from consciousness. This process feeds the soul with poison. She will starve because the avoided truth produces suffering.

Sometimes good intentions—"I'll hold my tongue, I don't want to hurt you," "Why stir things up?" "Best to leave well enough alone," and so many other well-known expressions—produce more harm than dealing with difficulties directly. In *The Visions Seminars,* Jung said the animus waits beneath the table for crumbs to fall and when they do this nourishment strengthens him enormously[79]. To feed the soul is to feed the heart.

In this sense, the soul is linked with the heart, organ traditionally associated to love. In *Psychological Commentary on Kundalini Yoga*, Jung affirms that the center of the heart (*anahata*) is where individuation begins, because at this stage of development of consciousness there is the possibility of putting oneself above emotional events and look at them. *Anahata* "is really the center where psychical things begin, [...] [where man] gets the first inkling of the power and substantiality, or the real existence, of psychical things"[80]. Symbolically it is in this center that a person can hold and support emotional difficulties without acting them out or repressing them. This process makes room for a greater capacity of symbolic elaboration, i.e., for the conscious experience that everything, without exception, even the most difficult emotions and the greatest wounds, possesses meaning beyond the obvious.

We see, thus, that Jung establishes a link between the world of depths, the soul, desire, and the heart—love, passion—while simultaneously seeking to discriminate between desire and the object of desire. This perception points to a loving experience that "is not only the longing for the Other, but is also an impulse to re-unite with oneself"[81]. The process revealed in the *Red Book* had its place within this universe.

Further along, Jung reinforces the idea that the anima appeared to him first in his dreams, adding that she made him undertake long, interminable journeys, and that he did not become frightened only because he was sure that she knew the way. And so, he asks who is the soul, since she appears in his dreams represented as a child and a maiden. Touched by this mystery, he asks her: "Are you God? Is God a child, a maiden?"[82].

The anima, perceived as mysterious, is represented as a child (for instance, in the dream of December 1912) and as a woman ("And I found you again only through the soul of the woman"[83]). But Jung goes further with his feelings, and asks the soul if she is God, here sketching the idea that he will develop throughout his work that the anima leads to the Self, to the Central Archetype. Through the image that represents the anima a man experiences totality and completeness, symbolized by the organizing center of the psyche. It is the experience of wholeness achieved through love.

Jung, who at this time was already a well-respected scientist, author of *Transformation and Symbols of the Libido,* invited to give seminars abroad, perceives that the knowledge of the heart brings more wisdom than scholarship. It requires experience not found in books or in purely rational teachings, but in a life fully lived. And so, Jung asks himself how he can obtain the knowledge of the heart, and he himself responds: "You can attain this knowledge only by living your life to the full"[84].

Jung reminds us of Faust's first speech in Goethe's work. He says:

> I've studied now Philosophy
> And Jurisprudence, Medicine,
> And even, alas! Theology,
> From end to end, with labor keen;
> And here, poor fool! With all my lore
> I stand, no wiser than before[85].

We can read the *Red Book* having as our Ariadne's thread the search for "the knowledge of the heart." The emergence of the archetype of the anima, theoretically defined by Jung as the unconscious feminine component in men, leads him to the heart, to the feeling function, to Eros. It is difficult to associate this mobilization, the backbone of *Liber Novus*, with the rupture between Jung and Freud, or even with the breakout of the First World War. The anima, Jung affirms, came to him "from the soul of woman." It is therefore appropriate to think of the experiences described in the *Red Book* as specially influenced by the presence of the woman who touched Jung's soul deeply: Toni Wolff.

Jung's process of surrendering to his deep self, to his soul (and we saw that, at this time, Jung identified the anima with God) through the loving relationship with a woman, did not happen without crises. He had to question what he had considered up to that moment to be his true self. Jung wrote that the spirit of this time permitted him to believe in his reason, in his most mature thoughts, making him feel like a leader. However, the spirit of the depths showed him his submission to the child, something he found distasteful, repugnant, but had to admit and accept. He felt, in fact, that his soul was a child, as well as his God[86].

This perception recalls Jesus' teachings: "Whomever will not receive the kingdom of God like a little child, will in no way enter into it" (Mark 10:15).

Jung further adds that men have a maiden as God[87], indicating that Jung's God is a child and also a woman. The image of God is one that imposes humility, reverence, and respect on us. For someone identified with reason, a scholar, a scientist like Jung, it was repugnant and detestable to surrender himself to a child, since it symbolizes the opposite of reason: abandonment, playfulness, spontaneity, irrationality, enthusiasm, involvement, emotion. Possibly his reactions regarding women were the same, especially if we consider that in Jung's time, and in the theory he later developed, it was believed that women had to pass through considerable elaboration and consciousness development in order to be able to think objectively, and not be easily caught up in *a priori* opinions based in subjective impressions or in needing acceptance and adaptation. Thus, the fact that God was represented by a woman demonstrates how much she carried an aura of transcendence and rapture for him.

If, on the one hand, Jung was disposed to follow the path proposed by the spirit of the depths and submit himself to his soul, on the other hand, through the whole process, his reluctance appears permeated by dread, hesitation, anguish, guilt, a feeling of being small, ridiculous, and the fear of going crazy. Accompanying Jung's reactions allows us to empathize with the suffering he experienced.

> Where are you leading me? Forgive my excessive apprehension, brimful of knowledge. My foot hesitates to follow you. [...] Must I also learn to do without meaning? If this is what you demand, then so be it. [...]. What is there, where there is no meaning? Only nonsense, or madness, it seems to me. Is there also a supreme meaning? Is that your meaning, my soul? I limp after you on crutches of understanding. I am a man and you stride like a God. What torture! I must return to myself to my smallest things. I saw the things of my soul as small, pitiably small. You force me to see them as large, to make them large. Is that your aim? I follow, but it terrifies me. Hear my doubts, otherwise I cannot follow, since your meaning is a supreme meaning, and your steps are the steps of a God.
>
> [...] I should give myself completely into your hands—but who are you? I do not trust you. Not once to trust, is that my love for you, my joy in you?
>
> [...] I must learn to love you. Should I also set aside self-.judgment? I am afraid. Then the soul spoke to me and said: "This fear testifies against me!" It is true, it testifies against you. It kills the holy trust between you and me.
>
> During six further nights, the spirit of the depths was silent in me, since I swayed between fear, defiance, and nausea, and was wholly the prey of my passion. I could not and did not want to listen to the depths. But on the seventh night, the spirit of the depths spoke to me: "Look into your depths, pray to your depths, waken the dead!"[88]

Jung used very strong expressions that reveal hesitation, fear, nonsense, terror, distrust, nausea as well as love and passion. According to Jung himself, the soul provokes a vivification of unconscious content and gives the "dead" the possibility of manifesting themselves[89]. This indicates that the passion that terrorized him, because it placed him against everything that is rational and reasonable, activated unconscious emotional content, which woke him to a new condition, to the very depths of his being.

In this sense, Jung confirms his need to know himself beyond his thoughts and his dedication to men and events. His thoughts, he perceives, kept him apart from his soul and made him feel desert-like, distant from events, from people, and from himself. Avoiding contact with his soul, he sought refuge in the distant realm led by thoughts, and from where he should depart in order to come closer to his own self[90].

This experience reinforces the idea that the unfolding of the process laid open in the *Red Book* has as its backbone the questioning of the thinking function as the protagonist of truth, and the development of the feeling function, which could not be mobilized without a very intense emotional experience.

Dominant traditional Western culture identifies man with force, with power, with command, and also with thought, with logic, objectivity and awareness. Thus feelings, emotions, affective relations, intuition and spontaneity were predominately associated with women. When Jung wrote his experiences, he lived at a time in which the stigmatization of these values was practically unquestioned. Not that these values have been radically modified nowadays, but there was, after the sexual revolution and the hippie movement with their slogans "Make Love, Not War," "Flower Power," and so many others, a greater acceptance of them by collective consciousness. Nevertheless, the development of the feeling function is, even today, a challenge for many men, as it was for Jung.

Jung took refuge in thought by turning from his desire for things and people. He became, then, prey of his thoughts, and concluded that he tried to distance himself from his desires by not thinking about them, but they only became more intense[91]. By trying to repress his desire, he fell victim to his thoughts and perceived that his mental life had become a desert, although his desires continued to burn. A bit later, he refers to the ancients who went to the desert in search of their souls[92].

The search to distance his desire from the world points perhaps to an attempt at sublimation, repression, or even negation, but maybe because it is a movement that runs against his essence, it ends up taking over his thoughts, that is, it emerges again with more force. And so, Jung recalls the ancients, those who went to the desert in search of their souls. Nevertheless, these old monks often went to the desert with celibatarian intentions, and with a disposition to face down the temptations of sexual desire. But it is desire that brings out creative force. And therein the proposal: to bring creative force to the soul. "If your creative force now turns to the place of the soul, you will see how your soul becomes green and how its field bears wonderful fruit"[93].

This movement can be seen not as repressing desire but as the creation of a container, of a receptacle, so that desire can be contained and transformed. This is the principle of Tantrism. Originating in India, this traditional form of yoga proposes the containment of desire, rather than its repression, as a pathway to spiritual development. However, one has to endure the inherent wait in this process, since the maturation period is not rapid. Still in the Hindu tradition, we find in the *Bhāgavata Purana* a type of erotic mysticism as a central religious idea[94].

The passage from impersonal sexuality to an amorous bond with a woman is a fundamental aspect of the *Minnedienst*, or love-service, from the times of courtly love developed alongside romanticism in the twelfth century. As in romantic love and in Tantrism, what emerges forcefully and with much attraction in Jung's process is the image of the anima. In these examples, they appear as woman: the damsel who must be saved by the knight, the Goddess in Tantrism, and the figure of Salome, with whom Jung will soon meet in his imagination—all are images of the anima that take man in the direction of his own being, to his essence, and to experiences of transcendence.

Love can bring with it numinous experiences, and in this sense they can also be religious experiences. With an impulse for synthesis and unification, love points to the realization of what one is potentially, to individuation, at the same time that it reveals the presence of something larger capable of transcending the ego. According to Guggenbühl-Craig[95], the mystic union with God is in part symbolized by the act of love. Love as an element that leads to divinity, plenitude, or wholeness, is well known in several cultures. However, the simple presence of love is not enough to make the individual grow, since it can also lead to indiscrimination, fascination, imprisonment, fanaticism, obsession.

Jung describes, then, what we perceive as different results originating, on the one hand, from acting out a desire or impulse and, on the other, the reflex of elaboration and containment of impulse or desire. He says that most people cannot endure the torture of waiting for desire to be transformed and to flow toward his or her soul, so as not to make the person a slave to the desired object. Jung adds: "The ancients lived their symbols, since the world had not yet become real for them"[96].

What does it mean that the world becomes real? Can we suppose that "real" in this context means existential, experiential? And what does not become real for them? What was lived only in the imagination, in fantasy? The ancients who isolated themselves in the desert were going to meditate, pray, distance themselves from the world. Many times they made a vow of poverty and were ascetics.

In the desert, in isolation, in simplicity, in introversion, the ascetics encountered their imagination, were overwhelmed with visions and remained in contact with "the wondrous flowers of the soul"[97]. But internal images can only emerge if activated, constellated, to use a word dear to Jung. And the presence of unfulfilled love is a very strong stimulus to this.

Traditionally, the West considered the development of spirituality to be a path opposite to that of sexual experience. To get to the spirit, it was necessary to repress sex. The world that still had not become real to the ancients was a spiritual world that bore the transcendence of sexual experience. Saint Anthony thanked God for not being responsible for his dreams. The passage of sexuality to love is also a process of "depuration."

Love, like the pain it provokes, inspires even the non-poets. The absence of love even ends up taking more space in the soul than its realization. In its absence, it makes itself more present. The obstacles for the realization of love strengthen it.

In Jung's case, he was married and wanted to continue to be. But he also decided that he would surrender to love for Wolff (as we've seen, this decision came after a dream, in December 1912). The conflict and tension generated by the circumstances, combined with his intelligence, sensibility, interest in the psyche, and fidelity to his internal process were some of the ingredients mobilizing Jung. He does not hide his state of confusion, replenished with doubts. Even feeling the need to remain alone with his soul, in some moments Jung loses hope and confidence in himself, perceiving that he is without the necessary patience to endure the process.

> I had fallen into an undergrowth of doubt, confusion, and scorn. I recognize that I must be alone with my soul. [...] I would like to sit down near you and at least feel the breath of your animating presence. My way is hot sand. All day long, sandy, dusty paths. My patience is sometimes weak, and once I despaired of myself, as you know.
>
> [...] You are to me like a shady tree in the wilderness. I would like to enjoy your shade. But my soul answered, "You are pleasure-seeking. Where is your patience? Your time has not yet run its course. Have you forgotten why you went into the desert?"[98]

Although difficult to keep, patience is viewed as the path, in the same way it was seen by the ancient ascetics. When his soul tells him he is seeking pleasure and asks for patience, it demonstrates that pleasure does not want to wait for satisfaction. To delay requires sacrifice, capacity for abstraction to surpass the immediate satisfaction, in order to connect with what lies beyond. Delaying the realization of pleasure demands the ability to endure frustration, and to this end patience is a great help.

At the beginning of his process, Jung used metaphors associated with heat to describe what he was living: "experiences in the desert," "all day long, sandy, dusty paths," "you are to me like a shady tree in the wilderness. I would like to enjoy your shade," "the heat lies on me like lead. Thirst torments me"[99]. Fire is an element that produces heat and for this reason it is associated with a lot of energy. It is also a metaphor for impulse, initiative, desire, creativity, for what mobilizes, and, in this sense, for the great emotions, such as love, hate, passion, and aggression.

Fire possesses characteristics that permit us to consider it an element capable of transforming, when it is mild; of destroying, when it is very intense and out of control; and also, mythically, of authenticating something that has reached the ideal point of transformation, attaining its essential state. This attribute created the "test by fire"—we have the expression "put your hand in the fire"—and only the incorruptible come out the winners. As knavery belongs to the human kingdom, this test can be defrauded, as occurred in *Tristan and Isolde.*

Besides the desire and the emotions that he perceived he was living, Jung attributed some characteristics to the soul, among which were simplicity of the mind, associated with non-intentionality, an attribute that carries with it the possibility of conquering the soul. In contraposition, the spirit of this time made him consider himself clever, able to control and conquer the world[100]. Thus, on the one hand, the need for spontaneity, nature, to follow his inner call; on the other, the attempt to command nature, to attribute a paramount place in life to reason, to control and dominate his own self.

The Vision of December 12, 1913

On December 12, 1913, Jung has a vision:

> I see a gray rock face along which I sink into great depths. I stand in black dirt up to my ankles in a dark cave. Shadows sweep over me. I am seized by fear, but I know I must go in. I crawl through a narrow crack in the rock and reach an inner cave whose bottom is covered with black water. But beyond this I catch a glimpse of a **luminous red stone** which I must reach. I wade through the muddy water. The cave is full of the frightful noise of shrieking voices. I take the stone, it covers a dark opening in the rock. I hold the stone in my hand, peering around inquiringly. I do not want to listen to the voices, they keep me away. But I want to know. Here something wants to be uttered. I place my ear to the opening. I hear the flow of underground waters. I see the **bloody head of a man** on the dark stream. Someone wounded, someone slain floats there. I take in this image for a long time, shuddering. I see a large black scarab floating past on the dark stream.
>
> In the deepest reach of the stream **shines a red sun**, radiating through the dark water. There I see—and a terror seizes me—small serpents on the

> dark rock walls, striving toward the depths, where the sun shines. A thousand serpents crowd around, veiling the sun. Deep night falls. **A red stream of blood**, thick red blood springs up, surging for a long time, then ebbing. I am seized by fear. What did I see?[101] [emphasis mine]

A dark descent and, at the bottom of the abyss, a red stone; the bloody head of a man, "the hero"[102]; a sun in the darkness; serpents. Descent into the underworld, associated with the dark night of the soul, can be seen as an entrance into his personal darkness, into the unknown, into depression, and conflict. The encounter with the red stone, however, brings a contrast expressed by color: in the midst of the absence of color, a hot color, color of blood, color of the sun, color representing the vibrant emotions of passion and hate.

Jung associated the scarab with death and rebirth, as it was considered in ancient Egypt. To the sun arising from the depths, "full of riddles," he associated the awakening of the dead, in the same way that the springtime sun awakens the dead earth of winter. According to Jung the battle between light and darkness begins there[103].

Can we consider the sun that awakens the dead a symbol of light, of emotion, of Eros, of love, awaking a life that Jung judged dead? In 1913, Jung was 38 years old, an age that he characterized as mid-life. He said that, on this occasion, his unconscious needed liberation, since "the conscious became practically a *tabula rasa*, and the subjacent content had to be liberated"[104]. He added that the technique he used—active imagination—is only applicable when unconscious content is activated. "It is only when problems arise that we are forced into a conscious attitude toward our psychical processes"[105].

Jung's search for his soul led him to see the shimmer of the red stone, a symbol of the indestructible life. The yearning to feel ßalive connected to his essence and the meaning of life, distances Jung from the hegemony of reason and brings him closer to a scene filled with Dionysian elements. The cave is, traditionally, the location of Dionysos' cult; the serpent, according to Kerényi[106], is a life phenomenon, whose coolness, mobility, slippery character and, frequently, deathly threat, cause a highly ambivalent impression. The snake also represents the identity of *Zoë,* indestructible life, in its lowest form[107]. The earth's sun, from the depths, is Dionysos himself, "the light of Zeus"[108]. Jung emphasized, in the corrected draft, the references about the orphic representation of a stream of mud in the underworld[109].

The Orphics worshipped the first Dionysos (Zagreus), who was dismembered by the Titans. Zeus recovered his heart, and gave it to Semele in a drink, so that she would gestate it. With her death, Zeus placed Dionysos on his thigh, and from it the god was born, the second Dionysos—hence he is considered the god of death and rebirth. To protect him from Hera's fury, Hermes gave him to Ino, who, together with her husband, King Atamas, raised Dionysos as a girl[110]. His capacity to move between the worlds of both genders is attributed to his living among women, thus he is seen as an androgynous god, in the sense of being able to integrate both masculine and feminine elements in his personality.

Unlike Apollo, the sun god, representative of culture and civilization, Dionysos is associated with the mysteries of life and death, with vegetation, with consciousness associated with the depths, irrationality, a life fully lived, the emotions and sensuality that lead to an altered state of consciousness, and to transcendence through experience. Dionysos is considered the god of ecstasy and of enthusiasm, because his devotees, after a frenzied dance, "become enraptured," and then "the god merges into his adorer, through enthusiasm"[111].

In associating these elements Jung found the characters from the myth and cult of Dionysos in his imagination. We perceive that the tension between the spirit of this time and the spirit of the depths is the same as that which exists between the world of Apollo and of Dionysos—not that Apollo who, in his beginnings, was associated with the Moon and the Delphic oracle, but the Apollo who, with evolution, came to be considered a sun god[112]. It is with the force of these symbols that Jung struggles within himself. On the one hand, the importance he rationally gives to current values, adaptation to society, status, familial insertion, "civilization;" on the other hand, transgression, breaking with patterns, inner space opening up to the world of emotions, of feeling, of love, of spontaneous and "brute" nature. The conflict Jung lived reached enormous proportions, as we can gauge from the depth of the process revealed in the *Red Book.* As psychotherapists we recognize the anguish, fear, and the sense of threat that accompanies the entrance to the depth of being!

And then Jung asks his soul to cure the wounds that doubt has caused him, saying that he possesses a tormented spirit, a victim of thinking. He asks for help so as not to be suffocated by his own knowledge, and to be protected from judgment[113].

> I want to go down cleansed into your depths with white garments and not rush in like some thief seizing whatever I can and fleeing breathlessly.[114]

To suffocate oneself in one's own knowledge is to fall victim to thought, to the emotional distancing that it usually brings, to the judgment that distances one from life. In 1925, Jung amplifies the symbol of the serpent, considering it a magical animal before which one can hardly remain indifferent. "As I am an introverted intellectual my anima contains feeling [that is] quite blind. In my case, the anima contains [...] some of the serpent, which is sensation as well"[115].

> So whenever a snake appears, you must think of a primordial feeling of fear. The black color goes with this feeling, and also with the subterranean character of the snake. It is hidden and therefore dangerous. [...]; it is the instinctive movement or tendency; it shows the way to the hidden treasure, or it guards the treasure. [...] The snake has a fascinating appeal, a peculiar attraction through fear. Some people are fascinated by this fear. Things that are awe-inspiring and dangerous have an extraordinary attraction. [...] The serpent shows the way to hidden things and expresses the introverting, which leads man to go beyond the point of safety, and beyond the limits of consciousness, as expressed by deep crater.[116]

In Jung's process, surpassing the secure limit on the way to the unknown generates fear and attraction, and also brings on a sense of guilt. Here, he affirms wanting to go to the depths dressed in white and not rushing like a thief. In the dominant Western tradition, the white clothing is an initiation robe, since white symbolizes purity, a disposition for what is new, the immaculate, the future, and also the idea of peace. And this is Jung's disposition: to be initiated in the mysteries of the depths, in his most profound being, in his essential feelings, allowing himself to be transformed by them, considering them clean, clear, worthy, and not being seen as a thief, someone who commits a crime and who must be punished, or who seeks to hide himself, in order to conceal a suspicious action.

It is not hard for us to empathize with Jung's conflict: he wanted to be faithful to himself, but at the same time he had to confront the challenge of fidelity to his wife. They were different callings, conflicting paths, completely contrary to the precepts of the time. But wasn't this the challenge he faced when he introduced Wolff into his familial and professional life alongside Emma?

Belonging to a family of Swiss Reform education, to live adultery openly with Wolff in a society traditionally monogamous, meant taking on a great challenge. If the encounter with the woman he loved mobilized profound experiences, it also allowed him to advance in the process of individuation and provided innumerable theoretical discoveries. This could not occur without considerable conflict, torment, suffering, fear, guilt, ambiguity, and anguish, as we see throughout the *Red Book*.

> Take note of what the ancients taught us in images: madness is divine. [...] It is unquestionable: if you enter into the world of the soul, you are like a madman, and a doctor would consider you to be sick. What I say here can be seen as sickness, but no one can see it as sickness more than I do.
>
> [...]
>
> But who can withstand fear when the divine intoxication and madness comes to him? Love, soul, and God are beautiful and terrible.[117]

Jung's immersion in his culture left him dominated by the spirit of this time, and provoked in him a one-sidedness that his psyche did not accept, creating an *enantiodromia*, a leap toward its opposite, taking him to merge into the spirit of the depths. The association between love, soul, and God allows us to think of love as an element of openness to the world of the soul.

The impulse for knowledge, discovery, deepening, and union is activated by love and can be directed as much to the other as to oneself, or even to both. The experience of love does not occur with impunity. In its presence it is impossible not to be touched by it. Love as an element of union impels one toward totality and in this state God presents Himself. Thus, in the passage by Jung, it seems plausible to think that moved by love, he opened his soul and, thus, experienced the numinous, i.e., the feeling of been filled by the divine. The amorous encounter as a symbol of totality emerges in different epochs and places, as was demonstrated in my master's dissertation[118].

Shamdasani reveals what Jung wrote in the draft: "My soul is my supreme meaning, my image of God [...] God becomes apparent in the supreme meaning of the human community"[119].

Concerning the "divine madness," this theme was so important to Jung that he gave this title to one of the experiences described in the *Red Book*. In due course, we will amplify this theme.

Dream with Siegfried

In the December 12, 1913 vision, Jung stumbles upon the bleeding head of a murdered man. He writes, "the blond hero lay murdered"[120]. A few days later, on the 18th, he had the following dream—or vision[121]. I transcribe it below as it was described in the *Red Book*[122], noting in square brackets the complementary description made in *Memories, Dreams, Reflections*[123].

> I was with a [an unknown, brown-skinned] youth [a savage] in [a lonely, rocky] high mountains. It was before daybreak, the Eastern sky was already light [and the stars fading]. Then Siegfried's horn resounded over the mountains with a jubilant sound. We knew that our mortal enemy was coming [and I knew that we had to kill him]. We were armed and lurked beside a narrow rocky path to murder him. Then we saw him coming high across the mountains [in the first ray of the rising sun] on a chariot made of the bones of the dead. He drove boldly and magnificently over the steep rocks and arrived at the narrow path where we waited in hiding. As he came around the turn ahead of us, we fired at the same time and he fell slain [struck dead]. [Filled with disgust and remorse for having destroyed something so great and beautiful,] I turned to flee, [impelled by the fear that the murder might be discovered]. A terrible rain swept down [and I

knew it would wipe out all traces of the dead]. But after this I went through a torment unto death and I felt certain that I must kill myself if I could not solve the riddle of the murder of the hero. [I had escaped the danger of discovery; life could go on, but an unbearable feeling of guilt remained.]

In the 1925 seminars, Jung offers some more details about this material, saying that they (Jung and the brown-skinned youth) shot at Siegfried's chest.

> The little man with me went forward, and I knew he was going to drive the knife into Siegfried's heart, but that was just a little too much for me, and I turned and fled. I had the idea of getting away as fast as I could to a place where "they" could not find me. I had the choice of going down into the valley or further up the mountains by a faint trail. I chose the latter, and as I ran there broke upon me a perfect deluge of rain. Then I awoke with a sense of great relief.[124]

Shamdasani, in a footnote, calls attention to the fact that Jung wrote a continuation of this dream/vision in the *Black Book* 2, on page 57:

> I strode light-footedly up an incredibly steep path and later helped my wife, who followed me at a slower pace, to ascend. Some people mocked us, but I didn't mind, since this showed that they didn't know that I had murdered the hero.[125]

The number of times Jung mentioned this dream—or this vision—and its elaboration over the years show its enormous importance to his process of individuation. He gave great prominence to the symbol of Siegfried, since he is the central hero of Nordic and German mythologies. Jung wrote about him in the *Red Book*:

> Oh that Siegfried, blond and blue-eyed, the German hero, had to fall by my hand, the most loyal and courageous! He had everything in himself that I treasured as the greater and more beautiful; he was my power, my boldness, my pride. I would have gone under in the same battle, and so only assassination was left to me. If I wanted to go on living, it could only be through trickery and cunning.
>
> [...]

What does Siegfried mean for the Germans! What does it tell us that the Germans suffer Siegfried's death! That is why I almost preferred to kill myself in order to spare him. But I wanted to go on living with a new God.[126]

In 1925, Jung referred to Siegfried in the following manner:

Siegfried was not an especially sympathetic figure to me, and I don't know why my unconscious got engrossed in him. Wagner's Siegfried, especially, is exaggeratedly extraverted and at times actually ridiculous. I never liked him. Nevertheless my dream showed him to be my hero. I could not understand the strong emotion I had with the dream.[127]

And he continues:

The hero [...] is the greatest value recognized by us. [...] So it appeared as if Siegfried were my hero. I felt an enormous pity for him, as though I myself had been shot. I must then have had a hero I did not appreciate, and it was my ideal of force and efficiency I had killed. I had killed my intellect, helped on to the deed by a personification of the collective unconscious, the little brown man with me. In other words, I deposed my superior function. [...]

The rain that fell is a symbol of the release of tension; that is, the forces of the unconscious are loosed. When it happens, the feeling of relief is engendered. The crime is expiated because, as soon as the main function is deposed, there is a chance for other sides of the personality to be born into life.[128]

He returns to this dream in *Memories, Dreams, Reflections:*

When I awoke from the dream, I turned it over in my mind, but was unable to understand it. I tried therefore to fall asleep again, but a voice within me said, "You *must* understand the dream, and must do so at once!" The inner urgency mounted until the terrible moment came when the voice said, "If you do not understand the dream, you must shoot yourself!" In the drawer of my night table lay a loaded revolver, and I became frightened. Then I began pondering once again, and suddenly the meaning of the dream dawned on me. "Why, that is the problem that is being played out in the world." Siegfried, I thought, represents what the Germans want

> to achieve, heroically to impose their will, have their own way. "Where there is a will there is a way!" I had wanted to do the same. But now that was no longer possible. The dream showed that the attitude embodied by Siegfried, the hero, no longer suited me. Therefore it had to be killed.
>
> After the deed I felt an overpowering compassion, as though I myself had been shot: a sign of my secret identity with Siegfried, as well as of the grief a man feels when he is forced to sacrifice his ideal and his conscious attitudes. This identity and my heroic idealism had to be abandoned, for there are higher things than the ego's will, and to these one must bow.[129]

As we can see, Jung interpreted Siegfried as content to be overcome and, therefore, killed. For Jung, the hero must die for our redemption. Paradoxically, Jung says he functions as a model to be imitated[130]. A hero represents an ideal or conscious attitude before the world that, in this case, should be abandoned so that one's personality might continue to develop. Jung mentions his principal function of consciousness, his ideal of force and efficiency, and his intellect as expressions contained in the symbol of the murdered hero. From this perspective we can think about Siegfried's death as an attempt to surpass his syntony with the "spirit of this time." Furthermore, in the years following his entrance in the Burghölzli, Jung was called "Our Siegfried"[131].

We remember also that, in the myth, Siegfried was Sigmund's son. And at the time of the dream, Jung was in the process of rupturing relations with Sigmund Freud, with whom he had an intense and beneficial collaborative relationship despite their enormous difficulties, permeated by the affective complexes of both[132] and by the presence of ambiguities in relation to their father-son dynamic (Freud was 19 years older than Jung). This imminent separation also threatened Jung's clinic.

There was, however, something in the Siegfried symbol that Jung didn't mention, but that comes to us thanks to Carotenuto's work[133]. As we know, Sabina Spielrein and Jung had an amorous relationship between 1904 and 1909. Spielrein studied medicine and became an analyst, having been a member of the psychoanalytic group. In 1912, she wrote *Destruction as the Cause of Coming into Being*. This article was published jointly with the first half of Jung's work *Transformation and*

Symbols of the Libido, in *Jahrbuch*, a journal edited by Jung.

Siegfried was the name of the son that Spielrein had fantasized she would have with Jung. This symbol was so vital for her that, although they had broken off their personal relationship in 1909, in the last known letter that she wrote to Jung, in 1918, she continued to elaborate Siegfried's meaning with him. Of the various references that Spielrein makes of Siegfried, some seem worth bringing up here. The following passage was taken from the letter she wrote to Jung when she sent him the above-mentioned work.

> Receive now the product of our love, the project which is your little son Siegfried. It caused me tremendous difficulty, but nothing was too hard if it was done for Siegfried.[134] (Letter probably written during the early months of 1912)

In a long letter sent to Jung, dated January 6, 1918, Spielrein further elaborates the Siegfried symbol and writes:

> [...] you finally killed off the "real" Siegfried, as you explained it to me (proof that you, too, had a "real" one), i.e., sacrificed him in favor of a sublimated one.[135]

Although we do not know the date in which Jung "explained it" to Spielrein, her statement shows that "Siegfried" was also present in his psychic life.

Their relationship was important for Jung as well, who, in 1919, after the experiences of 1913 and 1914, which were described in the *Red Book*, and their later elaboration, writes to Spielrein:

> The love of S. to J. made the latter aware of something he had previously only vaguely suspected, that is, of a power in the unconscious that shapes one's destiny, a power which later led him to things of the greatest importance. The relationship had to be "sublimated" because otherwise it would have led him to delusion and madness (the concretization of the unconscious). Occasionally one must be unworthy, simply in order to be able to continue living. (Letter by Jung to Sabina written on September 1, 1919)[136].

Thus, in Jung's dream, Siegfried can also be considered the product of a clandestine love, a symbol that greatly mobilized Jung and filled him with dread. Killing him would be a way to destroy the threat coming from the spirit of the depths, which would bring Jung another great love. The hero had to die because he would have obligated Jung to behave heroically, facing everything and everyone who represented the spirit of this time: status, family, marriage, children, reputation, and Zurich's puritanical bourgeois society.

It's important to point out that Jung and the youth had killed the hero with a shot in the chest, or that the youth stabbed him in the heart, the organ representing love in our tradition[137]. The youth who helped him to kill the symbol of love could be that aspect of Jung's personality to which Spielrein refers in her diary:

> He [Jung] told me that he loves me for my magnificent, proud character, but he also told me that he would never marry me because he harbors within himself a great philistine who craves narrow limits and the typical Swiss style. (Written November 9, 1910) [138]

Also in Siegfried's image can be seen the evocation of a turbulent period experienced by Jung, which, at the time of this dream repeats itself by synchronicity.

In 1908, the tension between Jung and Bleuler[139] was growing, and Jung was preparing to leave the Burghölzli after 8 years of work[140]. His extramarital relationship with Spielrein became more intimate[141], and Jung proposed to live with her as he later did with Wolff:

> True, he [Jung] wanted to introduce me in his house, make me his wife's friend, but understandably his wife wanted no part of this business, so that "*volens-nolens*" most of it had to be kept secret from her (September 11, 1910) [142].

We must add to his professional crisis and to the conflict and pain that came from his adultery, the fact that his wife Emma gave birth to his son Franz in November 1908.

We should remember that the Siegfried dream/vision occurs in December 1913. In January of that same year, Jung and Freud broke off their personal relationship and headed toward a break in their professional relationship, which would not happen without a professional (and possibly affective) loss for Jung. He was now also affectionately involved with Wolff, a situation that certainly engendered enormous conflict and guilt especially because, at that time, Emma was again pregnant—in the sixth month of her fifth pregnancy.

The similarity between these two periods is, therefore, unequivocal.

For this reason, our attention is drawn to the fact that only in the *Black Book* 2 does Jung write that his wife was in this dream. This fact, omitted by Jung every time he related this dream to which he gave such extraordinary importance, only came to light thanks to Shamdasani's careful research[143].

After the hero had been killed with the youth's assistance—the clandestine love, which he felt threatened his sanity, his marriage, and his persona, murdered by the representation of an aspect that might be associated with the poverty in which he lived as a youth—Jung helps his wife to climb the mountain, not caring about the people that mocked them, "since this showed that they didn't know that I had killed the hero." That is, his marriage, his family, and his social status were preserved, which gave him a great sense of relief. In his memoirs, Jung emphasizes the importance that his family and his work always had for him.

It's curious that, after Jung had written that he would like to go down into the depths in white garments, and not like a thief on the run, he had to hide so that his transgression would not be discovered. Nevertheless, guilt was inevitable: "I had escaped the danger of discovery; life could go on, but an unbearable feeling of guilt remained"[144].

Jung mentioned the "torment unto death" through which he still passed, feeling that he should kill himself, "if I could not solve the riddle of the murder of the hero," shows that the problem suggested by the dream urgently demanded an elaboration. The hero announces himself by horn, with a festive sound. At the same time, he comes on a chariot made of the bones of dead people, which he easily drives. Joy comes associated with death. The bones could represent necessary destruction so that a new life could emerge. In Jung's situation the bones could refer to the destruction of his marriage, his status quo, so that his life with Wolff could be lived freely. However, breaking with traditional values, with his social and financial position, and with his family, especially when a new child was about to be born, would have been something very violent for Jung. And so the conflict is "solved" with the murder of Siegfried, he who brings death also carries sensibility, love and life. Jung's "philistine" aspect would temporarily win out, since he was still unable to accept a "change in destiny."

An observation made by Henry Murray, a Jung analysand, makes clear that Jung was syntonic with the spirit of this time, with its morals, values, and customs. Murray affirms that Jung had said, regarding his relation with Wolff: "It isn't good in a moral sense, but it has to be"[145]. To include Wolff in his life afterwards was certainly the result of overcoming collective values and the enormous tension, from which Jung's disposition to seek "higher things than the ego's will" emerged victorious.

Guilt and Elaboration

After his dream with Siegfried, Jung wrote: "Through guilt I have become a newborn"[146]. In a footnote, Shamdasani shares commentary made by Jung in 1916, from the seminars given at the Psychology Club, about the importance of guilt: "The first step in individuation is tragic guilt"[147].

Siegfried's death provokes in Jung the awareness of the emergence of a new God, a divine child full of paradoxes—good and bad, serious and ridiculous, healthy and sick—that finds him disturbed by pain and by laughter, yes and no, and so, Jung understands that the new God is not to be found in the absolute, but in the relative[148].

> When my prince had fallen, the spirit of the depths opened my vision and let me become aware of the birth of the new God.
>
> The divine child approached me out of the terrible ambiguity, the hateful-beautiful, the evil-good, the laughable-serious, the sick-healthy, the inhuman-human and the ungodly-godly.
>
> I understood that the God whom we seek in the absolute was not to be found in absolute beauty, goodness, seriousness, elevation, humanity or even in godliness. Once the God was there.

I understood that the new God would be in the relative[149].

And further along, Jung writes:

> When the hero was slain and the meaning recognized in the absurdity; when all tension came rushing down from gravid clouds, when everything had become cowardly and looked to its own rescue, I became aware of the birth of the God. Opposing me, the God sank into my heart when I was confused by mockery and worship, by grief and laughter, by yes and no[150].

Jung is overwhelmed with pain and guilt for the death of the hero, symbol of love. He compares his suffering with Christ's in Hell when he says: "No one knows what happened during the three days Christ was in Hell. I have experienced it"[151]. The experience of *katabasis*, the decent into hell, brought forth in Jung the perspective of a new consciousness, in which relativity of opposites could be the center. With this, his attachment to tradition, norms, and collective values could give way to that which belonged to his deepest self. And thus, he associates hell's exit to "beauty and joy came over men when the depths unleashed this greatest war"[152]. Here is the seed not only of important theoretical conceits, such as Self (Central Archetype), shadow, the principle of polarities, and the process of individuation, but also of his personal awakening to the integration of Eros and feeling in his personality.

> What do you think of the essence of Hell? Hell is when the depths come to you with all that you no longer are or are not yet capable of. Hell is when you can no longer attain what you could attain. Hell is when you must think and feel and do everything that you know you do not want. Hell is when you know that your having to is also a wanting to, and that you yourself are responsible for it. Hell is when you know that everything serious that you have planned with yourself is also laughable, that everything fine is also brutal, that everything good is also bad, that everything high is also low, and that everything pleasant is also shameful.
>
> But the deepest Hell is when you realize that Hell is also no Hell, but a cheerful Heaven, not a Heaven in itself, but in this respect a Heaven, and in that respect a Hell.[153]

Jung's openness to the polarities, to the "ambiguity," also permits him to elaborate the paradox of love. He writes:

> [...] But ambiguity is the way of life. [...]
>
> You say: the Christian God is unequivocal, he is love. But what is more ambiguous than love? Love is the way of life, but your love is only on the way of life if you have a left and a right.
>
> Nothing is easier than to play at ambiguity and **nothing is more difficult than living ambiguity.** He who plays is a child; his God is old and dies. He who lives is awakened; his God is young and goes on. He who plays hides from the inner death. He who lives feels the going onward and immortality. So leave the play to the players. Let fall what wants to fall; if you stop it, it will sweep you away. There is a true love that does not concern itself with neighbors.[154] (emphasis mine)

Here is the central point of Jung's process of individuation, as it is described in the *Red Book*. How to live the ambiguity of love, when it is expressed in concrete relation to two women? Spielrein writes about Jung in a letter to Freud, on June 12, 1909: "his soul is constantly torn between two women"[155].

As for the phrase, "There is a true love that does not concern itself with neighbors," we can understand it as love for the process of individuation, love for the deepest dimension of the being, love that does not "play at ambiguity," but because it cries for realization—which, in this case, means self-realization—can hurt the Other. In Jung's situation, it's not hard to empathize with Emma's suffering.

Barbara Hannah, Jungian analyst who had a close relationship with Jung, Emma, and Wolff, believed that it was difficult for Jung, precisely when he was being tested by his "confrontation with the unconscious," to have to face a tremendously difficult problem for a married man: to love his wife and another woman at the same time. She considered, however, that these two situations were, in fact, two sides of the same coin[156].

The problem that Jung needed to elaborate was his love for Wolff. According to Murray, Jung had said that Wolff had an "uncanny ability to bring to light material from his unconscious that had been 'hidden back there under the crust of convention' "[157]. Probably, it was her capacity to trigger such profound and authentic emotional experiences in him that originated the material published in the *Red Book*.

In his Introduction to the *Red Book*, Shamdasani states that it's not an exaggeration to claim that if there were no war, the *Red Book* wouldn't exist[158], to which I respond: if the passion for Toni Wolff had not existed, *Liber Novus* would probably not have been written.

His relationship with Wolff activated psychic content in Jung that he would later on conceive as the anima archetype. This mobilized him with such intensity that it produced experiences of totality and transcendence in him and, because of this, at first he identified his soul with God—in theoretical terms, the anima with the Self, or the Central Archetype[159].

Elijah and Salome

Around the 20th December, 1913, Jung had another vision (active imagination), in which an old man, a beautiful young girl, and a black serpent appear to him. The old man looks like a prophet and introduces himself as Elijah. The girl, Salome, is his blind daughter.

These figures are among the most important of the *Red Book*, and Jung mentions them many times: in the 1925 seminars, in *Memories, Dreams, Reflections*, while also interpreting them in the corrected draft of the *Red Book* itself, published in Appendix B.

Elijah and Salome are biblical figures. He is precursor to and inspiration for the monastic life, symbol of the ascetic. He lives like a hermit in the desert, fighting against his worldly desires and seeking to serve God. It is worth observing that Jung, before Elijah's appearance, had mentioned the ancients who went to the desert in search of their souls. Maybe Elijah is the best personification of this solitary quest and of the sacrificial disposition inherent to his attitude. He is considered the precursor of Saint John the Baptist.

Salome, in her turn, was responsible for the death of John the Baptist. After dancing for her stepfather, Herod, he promises to satisfy her one wish, whatever that may be. Influenced by her mother, Herodias, whom the prophet had censured for living with her brother-in-law, Salome asks for the head of John the Baptist.

These figures call our attention for the polarity that they constitute: an ascetic prophet and a killer dancer, who enchanted her stepfather with her erotic gift.

Jung would associate the manifestation of the Wise Old Man Archetype, or of the Self, as Central Archetype, to Elijah, and the expression of the archetype of the anima to the figure of Salome. He also associated Logos and Eros to them, respectively. Nevertheless, he states in his memoirs, "such a definition would be excessively intellectual. It is more meaningful to let the figures be what they were for me at the time—namely, events and experiences"[160].

We must remember that the essence of the content transcribed in the *Red Book* in Gothic script spanned only four or five months, from October 1913 to February 1914. The quantity of material produced by Jung in this short time is an indication of the intensity of his emotional mobilization.

In the encounter with Elijah and Salome, described under the title, "Mysterium. Encounter," we have Salome's direct question, her first words directed to Jung: "Do you love me?"[161] Love's problem is brought by the personification of a woman who, by virtue of her eroticism, holds great destructive power.

I have had opportunity to hear many dreams and spontaneous images throughout my professional life, and I don't stop marveling at the creativity of the Central Archetype in producing its symbols. Perfect metaphors to reveal, to point the way, to translate what each one needs for her or his individuation process. It wouldn't be different with Jung. The images that we now know were, certainly, the best expression of his development process.

As the son of a protestant minister, biblical figures were part of Jung's formation. In the religious context, Salome represents a terrible, bloody, willful, cold, seductive, erotic woman. She is the shadow of the anima, capable of fascinating as well as destroying. Could there have been a better image to represent the fear, fascination, and, at the same time, attraction Jung felt for Wolff? With her, he discovers the anima—not because he hadn't lived it before, but because with Wolff he gives continuity to the process that was interrupted with Spielrein. This courage to move ahead with love, despite conflict, guilt, tension, anguish, and despair, took him where he had never been before, leading him to the creation of the concept of anima, by recognizing her within himself.

Salome, however, is blind. She was not in the myth, but she appeared thus in Jung's image. She who represented his anima, who initiated him in the deep elaboration of love, was considered blind. So, we can ask ourselves: what was Jung unable to see? A possible answer to this question is that in projecting blindness on his representation of Eros, he was blind to his own capacity for love. In counterpoint, clarity was projected on the personification of Elijah, prophet, ascetic, in line with the reign of the spirit, a representation of Logos. The blindness Jung attributes to Salome deprives her of plenitude, making her less worthy than Elijah. This shows more differentiated thinking than feeling, the spirit of this time devaluing the spirit of the depths.

As we've already mentioned, Jung stated: "As I am an introverted intellectual my anima contains feeling [that is] quite blind"[162]. And, in the *Red Book* itself, he writes: "pleasure is blind"[163].

One must also recall the segment of Jung's letter to Spielrein in which he affirms: "The relationship [between them] had to be 'sublimated' because otherwise it would have led him to delusion and madness (the concretization of the unconscious)." Here he establishes a connection between the love relationship (passion) and the fear of becoming blind by love and crazy with passion.

Salome insists on love, saying that Jung will love her and that she loves him. He, however, refuses this possibility, declaring that he feels horror for her and thinks her temptation is demonic. The dialog occurring between Jung and Salome suffers from the interference of Elijah, who asks Jung if he is a coward and announces that through her love he will know her. He adds that he is one with his daughter since eternity. Although Jung sees, he does not understand the extreme contradiction contained in the union of a prophet and a murderess[164].

> What my eyes see is exactly what I cannot grasp. You, Elijah, who are a prophet, the mouth of God, and she, a bloodthirsty horror. You are the

symbol of the most extreme contradiction.[165]

Although "in nature intimately one"[166], Elijah and Salome are contrasting, as "forethinking" (Elijah) and "pleasure" (Salome). We know that the more an element of the psyche is repressed, the more it will appear with characteristics of the shadow. The image of Jung's anima contains the negative dimension of Salome, which is capable of attracting, horrifying, and terrifying him, a reflex of the repression to which her meaning was submitted, not only in his personality but also in the time in which he lived. According to Jung, the anima opens space for man's sensitivity, for his lovingness and tenderness, what includes his capacity to love. We know that the problem of the elaboration of the anima (and animus) greatly influences collective consciousness and deeply interferes with relations between the sexes.

Jung, however, was courageous enough to face his fear, and continues to seek the integration of his anima throughout the whole process described in the *Red Book*. This elaboration is already noted when, in the sequence of the dialog summarized above, he writes that he is torn by doubt and questions himself about his identity with Salome, about his love for her—after all, does he fear her? Does he love her? Does he not love her? Should he love her? Was it for the sake of her love that he killed the hero?

> Doubt tears me apart. [...] Salome loves me, do I love her? I hear wild music, a tambourine, a sultry moonlit night, the bloody-staring head of the holy one—fear seizes me. [...] Who murdered the hero? Is this why Salome loves me? Do I love her, and did I therefore murder the hero? She is one with the prophet, one with John, but also one with me? Woe, was she the hand of the God? I do not love her, I fear her. Then the spirit of the depths spoke to me and said: "Therein you acknowledge her divine power." Must I love Salome?[167]

In asking for the head of John the Baptist, who was against the union between her mother and her uncle, Salome proposes, symbolically, that the head, metaphor for rationality, for thinking, for traditional moral and religious values, were separated from the body, as if in this way the body might be released from the yoke of repression and express itself freely.

She herself was a dancer: through her dance she was able to seduce and enchant Herod to the point of acquiring the power to kill John the Baptist. This defensive gesture can be seen as a reflex of the tension between the patriarchal moralistic tradition represented by John the Baptist, and Eros, the matriarchal sensuality, the pleasure and flexibility of customs, represented by Salome and her mother, Herodias.

The death of Siegfried was necessary so that Jung could perceive the importance of love; in this sense, becoming a murderer, he could be compared with Salome. The analogy between Salome and Jung continues when we see, among the images of Jung on December 12, 1913, a bloodied head of a man—after all, Jung's inner struggle is for the head to open space for the heart!

When Jung asks himself: "Do I love her, and did I therefore murder the hero?" we can answer in the affirmative. He killed the hero in an attempt to repress his own love, precisely because he felt it.

For Jung, the experience with Elijah and Salome was one of approximation to chaos, and the serpent, according to himself, shows that "my next step leads to pleasure and from there again on lengthy wanderings like Odysseus"[168]. As we know, Odysseus had to overcome the song of the sirens—the seduction of the defensive anima—to return from Troy.

In his elaborations of this vision, Jung writes: "The bright garden is the space of pleasure. He who lives there needs no vision; he feels the unending"[169]. Salome's vision is shown to be unnecessary at this time because she feels. Through pleasure, she feels the infinite! It is the realization that feeling and pleasure can lead to the experience of plenitude.

If, on the one hand, Jung considers thinking a protection against error, on the other he perceives that it leads to petrification. Therefore, a thinker must fear Salome, once she activates his anima, mobilizes his feelings, and he, emotionally immature, not knowing how to react in the face of it, "loses his head"[170]. He notes: "Thinking protects against the way of error, and therefore it leads to petrification."

> A thinker should fear Salome, since she wants his head, especially if he is a holy man. A thinker cannot be a holy person, otherwise he loses his head. […]

> [...] He who prefers to think than to feel, leaves his feeling to rot in darkness. It does not grow ripe [...][171]

And so he states: "In the garden it had to become apparent to me that I loved Salome. This recognition struck me, since I had not thought it"[172]. Jung recognizes his love through an unexpected means, since it wasn't through his thought. He recognizes love by feeling it! And the following night (December 22, 1913) he experiences another active imagination with Elijah and Salome. Elaborating it, Jung writes: "It is no small matter to acknowledge one's yearning"[173].

Jung shows the difficulty of being faithful to his yearning, the honesty required for this process and the necessity to face fear before the impossibility and/or the suffering that it can bring. It is easier to live the life of the collective, repeating teachings and fulfilling society's precepts and expectations, leaving aside the fear of solitude and defeat.

The capacity to evolve amorously and to open oneself to the world of feelings and relationships was, culturally, associated with and attributed to women. To men belonged Logos, logic, thinking, objectivity, and reason. This compartmentalization continues nowadays, although we now see a greater exchange between the attributes designated as belonging to men or to women.

Living his metanoia at the beginning of the twentieth century, Jung was culturally influenced by these stereotypes. A scholar, he valued thinking, reason, and Logos to the detriment of feeling, emotion, and Eros. In line with the spirit of this time, the search for his soul and the integration of his sensibility, Eros, and his capacity to love, elements present in the spirit of the depths, demanded of him a Herculean effort, as we've witnessed in the pages of the *Red Book*.

Here is an outline of the idea that grounded his notion of the individuation process:

> If you give up your self you live it in others; thereby you become selfish to others, and thus you deceive others. [...] To live oneself means: to be one's own task. Never say that it is a pleasure to live oneself. It will be no joy but a long suffering, since you must become your own creator.[174]

The transformation that he feels is happening does not occur by will, but as an "unavoidable effect." "I lock the past with one key; with the other I open the future"[175]. The future that emerges is one that will permit the union of opposites, the non-exclusion of internal truth in favor of adapting to the external world. "The way of life is transformation, not exclusion. Well-being is a better judge than the law"[176].

In other words, the future will permit the integration of polarities that were being experienced unilaterally. Instead of this or that, the future points to this *and* that. The ability to conjugate the polarities and establish between them a dialectic, non-hierarchical functioning is the expression of the alterity archetype, described by Carlos Byington in his book *Jungian Symbolic Psychology*. The alterity sought by Jung finds full expression in paradox, as is so well illustrated by the following passage:

> He who wants to accept himself must also really accept his other. But in the yes not every no is true, and in the no every yes is a lie. But since I can be in the yes today and in the no tomorrow, yes and no are both true and untrue.[177]

One of the great polarities to be integrated by Jung is that represented by the spirit of this time and the spirit of the depths, linked among other things, respectively, to Logos and Eros, thinking and feeling, collective values and values of individuation. Thus, when Jung perceives the freedom that exists beyond the world of thinking, Salome embraces him and he becomes a prophet who feels pleasure and recognizes that his pleasure is "the daughter of love"[178].

December 25, 1913

On this day, Jung longs anew for the mystery that he experienced in his encounter with Elijah and Salome. He meets Elijah. He sees Christ in His torment at the top of a mountain, and sees himself encircled by a serpent. Salome comes close and tells him that he is Christ. Jung, then, remains with his arms opened, blood gushing from his body. Salome bends over his feet and covers them with her black hair, staying that way for a long time. Suddenly, she screams that she sees light. Her eyes can see again! Elaborating the passage summarized here, Jung writes:

> My pleasure was with forethinking and had its merry garden there, surrounded by darkness and night. I climbed down to my pleasure, but ascended to my love. I see Elijah high above me: this indicates that forethinking stands nearer to love than I, a man, do. Before I ascend to love, a condition must be fulfilled, which represents itself as the fight between two serpents. Left is day; right is night. The realm of Love is light, the realm of forethinking is dark [...] Forethinking is singleness, love is togetherness. Both need one another, and yet they kill one another.[179]

With honesty, fidelity, and the capacity to penetrate the intimate truth of his being, Jung sets out in search for his soul, his pleasure, his love, the spirit of the depths. The experience related above, in which Christ plays a fundamental role, occurs by synchronicity on Christmas day. The scene in which Jung with his arms opened on top of the mountain, a snake wrapped around his body from which blood streams, experiencing self-sacrifice, while Salome kneels at his feet, covering them with her hair, immediately evokes the image of Mary Magdalene drying the Lord's feet with her hair. And Jesus pardons her for her sins because "she loved greatly" (Lc 7:47). Love redeems, and for this reason Salome recovers her vision.

Sacrificing himself for love, like Christ on the cross, Jung gives us a dimension of the suffering he was going through. He associates the struggle between the snakes with the tension that he had had to endure—on the one hand, thinking, reasoning, keeping his marriage in tune with society and its traditional values; on the other, adulterous love, emotion, transgression, individuation. His disposition to face suffering in order to develop his Eros, his capacity to love, results in Salome recovering her sight—love and thinking come to be considered equally important and, therefore, capable of provoking an internal war, in case one of them wished to impose itself upon the other. Jung writes:

> If you go to thinking, take your heart with you. If you go to love, take your head with you. Love is empty without thinking, thinking hollow without love. [...] Great is he who is in love [...][180].

Jung reaffirms his insertion in the spirit of his time, thinking and desiring like someone tuned in with it. However, thanks to his initiation in the mysteries of the spirit of the depths, he opens himself to readopt what was rejected in actuality and to reintegrate in his life that which belonged to Antiquity—to the world before it was dominated by reason—since without feeling he knows he will not have a full life. He recognizes that the spirit of his time has nothing more to offer him, because it had distanced him from the reality of his soul[181]. He affirmed, once again, the need he felt to conciliate the opposites in himself, bringing together what seemed excluding, like the divine and the mundane.

> [...] love, which is higher than pleasure, which however is still in me hidden in pleasure. [...] Pleasure always wants what is closest, and feels through the multiplicity; going from one to another, without a goal, just seeking and never fulfilled. Love wants what is furthest, the best and the fulfilling.[182]

When Jung declares that love, although higher than pleasure, is hidden in it, he reveals in his individuation process how he tuned in with his time, revealing that his problem is that of his culture—men who relate to women for sexual pleasure and not for love.

Jung went a step forward in elaborating this question when he affirmed that pleasure is transformed by self-sacrifice through which pleasure elevates itself in the direction of love. "Love is sighted, but pleasure is blind. Both principles are one in the symbol of the flame"[183]—a flame that can be understood here as symbol of passion.

It is meaningful that Elijah had said to Jung: "Your work is fulfilled here. Other things will come. Seek untiringly, and above all write exactly what you see"[184], since the images of Elijah and Salome will only return at the end of the *Red Book*. Similar to the initial dream in analysis, the first part of the *Red Book*, *Liber Primus*, contains the prognosis of Jung's process of development. With frankness, he affirmed that he still did not possess that which the mystery had shown him, needing to advance more in order to integrate in his personality that which was glimpsed[185].

LIBER SECUNDUS

Behind the ordinary the eternal abyss yawns[186].

Reason and Emotion

Liber Secundus begins with a vision in which Jung finds himself in the highest tower of a castle, which indicates a distant position in relation to what occurs on the ground, in daily life. The tower represents reason, leading to distancing from emotions. Notwithstanding, he wore a green cape and a horn—the instrument played by Siegfried in his dream—hung over his shoulder. He then saw a red point coming near, a horseman, the Red One.

The figure of the red horseman brings to mind the Red Knight, who is part of the first adventures of Parsifal, the hero of the Grail. It is very meaningful, because Jung came to consider the myth of the Grail as a myth of Western man and, in this sense, also his myth[187].

In accordance with the book *The Grail Legend*, written by Emma Jung and Marie-Louise von Franz, the Red Knight almost always refers to emotional content with some autonomy. Right at the beginning, the Red One says that Jung thinks he is the demon—possibly due to his color. Jung considers him "worldly, something impudent, or exuberant, or—in fact—something pagan"[188], i.e., he sees in him aspects opposed to his own rationality and scholarship. In the end, the Red One reveals himself as the joy of the unexpected, the lightness of life, the joy of poets before penetrating the depths, the joy of someone who forgets himself[189].

> Not the secret joy in his thoughts and in his looking, but that strange joy of the world that comes unsuspected, like a warm southerly wind with swelling fragrant blossoms and the ease of living. You know it from your poets, this seriousness, when they expectantly look toward what happens in the depths, sought out first of all by the devil because of their springlike joy. [...] "Whoever tastes this joy forgets himself"[190].

This description can be associated with strong emotional reactions, including falling in love. It was Jung who stated, regarding the transformation of the figure of the demon: "When he appears red, he is of a fiery, that is, passionate nature, and causes wantonness, hate, or unruly love"[191]. The joy to which he had access gives Jung the courage to follow his path. In the corrected draft, he wrote:

> With this newly gained joy I took off on adventures without knowing where the way would lead. I could have known, however, that the devil always tempts us first through women. While I might have had clever thoughts as a thinker, it was not so in life. There I was even fatuous and prejudiced.[192]

This is another sign that the process unraveled in the *Red Book* was marked by the experience Jung had in dealing with thinking and his inability to relate to his emotions. In life, before women and the temptations that they could come to represent, intelligent thoughts disappeared and he felt like a fool. This is the general functioning of a man whose typology is predominately thinking. He can be brilliant culturally and rationally, but affectionately he can be compared to a fool, to someone prejudiced, with a serious rigidity and limitation in expressing his emotions.

In his next vision, on December 28, 1913, Jung finds himself in an old castle, whose owner is a scholar. Jung will spend the night there. When going to bed, he imagines that the owner has a beautiful daughter who remains hidden in the castle. He thinks: "a vulgar idea for a novel [...] but the romantic can be felt in every limb [...] Have I such a novelistic soul?"[193]. The young woman emerges in his imagination and then a dialogue begins between her and Jung. Contrary to what he believes, she affirms that the ultimate truths can only be found in the human, in banality, in what he considers vulgar[194]:

> Jung: "But tell me, what do you think of the divinity; of the so-called ultimate truths? I found it very strange to seek them in banality. According to their nature, they must be quite uncommon. [...]"
>
> She: "The more uncommon these highest truths are, the more inhuman must they be and the less they speak to you as something valuable or meaningful concerning human essence and being. Only what is human and what you call banal and hackneyed contains the wisdom that you seek."[195]

Once more, there is an implied idea that wisdom does not come from scholarship or from thought; the really important things come from experience, from daily and incarnate life. It is the perception that Eros, love, emotion, all that was considered feminine, could lead to the ultimate truth, although, in principle, these elements were held to be banal and less important. Later, she asks if he loves her, to which he responds yes, but unfortunately he is already married[196]. She says that she brought greetings from Salome and disappears, leaving red roses in her place.

The red roses, associated with passion, carry the perfume of flowers, to which Jung associated the "joy of the world that comes unsuspected"—the world of Eros and of love.

Jung continues: "If no outer adventure happens to you, then no inner adventure happens to you either"[197], showing that the path of development cannot occur without concrete, existential life. Thus, because he intensely lived outer things that greatly moved him, his inner life was so intense. Anyone who has fallen in love knows how this emotion activates profound content and often brings with it new and creative elements to be integrated in the personality. For Jung, the adventure was favored by the joy brought by the demon (by the Red One).

"I was smitten by the romantic. The romantic is a step backward. To reach the way; one must sometimes also take a few steps backward"[198]. Jung's reluctance to accept this feeling is expressed as a step backwards, although he admitted the possibility of it being a necessary step. By the way, Jung utilized throughout his work the expression *reculer pour mieux sauter* (retreat, to better spring forward).

Romanticism is also associated with the Middle Ages—"I returned to my middle ages where I was still romantic, and there I experienced the adventure"[199]. "I must catch up with a piece of the Middle Ages—within myself"[200]. But it is also the symbol of the "uncivilized": "Asceticism, inquisition, torture are close at hand and impose themselves"[201].

The Middle Ages exerted such a fascination in Jung that he felt it necessary to erect a construction, a tower, in which he could live as though he was in that period. He wrote:

> In the Tower at Bollingen it is as if one lived in many centuries simultaneously. The place will outlive me, and in its location and style it points

backward to things of long ago. There is very little about it to suggest the present. If a man of the sixteenth century were to move into the house, only the kerosene lamp and the matches would be new to him; otherwise, he would know his way about without difficulty. There is nothing to disturb the dead, neither electric light nor telephone.[202]

We can recall Jung's dream of the knight of the twelfth century, transcribed here earlier. There is another dream, described by Jung in *Memories, Dreams, Reflections*, in which the figure of a crusader also appears.

> I was in a region like the Alyscamps near Arles. There they have a lane of sarcophagi which go back to Merovigian times. In the dream I was coming from the city, and saw before me a similar lane with a long row of tombs. They were pedestals with stone slabs on which the dead lay. They reminded me of old church burial vaults, where knights in armor lie outstretched. Thus the dead lay in my dream, in their antique clothes, with hands clasped, the difference being that they were not hewn out of stone, but in a curious fashion mummified. I stood still in front of the first grave and looked at the dead man, who was a person of the eighteen-thirties. I looked at his clothes with interest, whereupon he suddenly moved and came to life. He unclasped his hands; but that was only because I was looking at him. I had an extremely unpleasant feeling, but walked on and came to another body. He belonged to the eighteenth century. There exactly the same happened: when I looked at him, he came to life and moved his hands. So I went down the whole row, until I came to the twelfth century—that is, to a crusader in chain mail who lay there with clasped hands. His figure seemed carved out of wood. For a long time I looked at him and thought he was really dead. But suddenly I saw that a finger of his left hand was beginning to stir gently.[203]

As already mentioned, the twelfth century was marked, among other things, by courtly love, through which men dedicated themselves to develop their sensibility, their romanticism, their capacity to love through poetry, song, and prose, and with this, to overcome the relations with women marked only, or principally, by sex and power. This movement can be understood as an effort to integrate the anima, and it is part of the individuation process described by Jung in his work. Here this movement is experienced and related by Jung in the discovery, in the difficulty and need to accept his romantic, or better, his feminine side. He writes:

> [...] if you remain with yourself as a man who is himself and not of the devil, then you will remember your humanity. You will not behave toward women *per se* as a man, but as a human being, that is to say; as if you were of the same sex as her.[204]

For man, to behave as a human being, as a person, in relation to women, implies relating to them as equals, without emphasis on a hierarchical relationship, which subjugates woman by force, by sex or by power, and that predominated and still predominates in our cultural tradition. From submissive housewives to women as object, each one, in her way, was deprived of her profound identity by this tradition.

Solitude, Death, and Rebirth

Jung's next steps took him to experience solitude, isolation, and death, and he is struck by a terrible cold. He sees the spirits of the dead—men, women, children, animals, insects, vegetables—a veritable sea of blood.

> And thus I went out in that night (it was the second night of the year 1914), and anxious expectation filled me. I went out to embrace the future. The path was wide and what was to come was awful. It was the enormous dying, a sea of blood. From it the new sun arose, awful and a reversal of that which we call day. We have seized the darkness and its sun will shine above us, bloody and burning like a great downfall.[205]

This passage of the *Red Book* brings forth an image of enormous destruction. The image came to Jung at the beginning of 1914, and he later interpreted it as a premonition of what was to come—the First World War. In fact, we know that dreams and visions can be premonitory, and the force with which Jung faced this devastating destruction—added to his visions of a bloody Europe—confirms this possibility. This experience was so intense for Jung that he considered what he described in the *Red Book* a consequence of this intuition.

After the image of this destruction, Jung understood his own darkness and from there emerged his phoenix.

> When I comprehended my darkness, a truly magnificent night came over me and my dream plunged me into the depths of the millennia, and from it my phoenix ascended.[206]

Death leading to rebirth is a recurrent theme of various myths, including the Christian myth. In Jung's process it was no different. The reborn phoenix that leads him to "a truly magnificent night" where he understands that his darkness can be thought of as overcoming the experience of solitude, anguish, and death when he opens himself up again to love.

The dynamic of approximation and withdrawal, encounter and search for solitude contained in *Liber Secundus* seems to mirror the conflict between surrendering to love and recoiling from it, and it reproduces as a sort of spiral the experience described in the *Liber Primus*, which passes sequentially through the chapters "Refinding the Soul," "The Desert," "Experiences in the Desert," and "Descent into Hell in the Future," leading to "Mysterium. Encounter."

> But it is the unacceptable, the awfully repulsive, that which I have forever rejected that rises in me. For if the wretchedness and poverty of this life ends, another life begins in what is opposed to me. This is opposed to such an extent that I cannot conceive it. For it is opposed not according to the laws of reason, but thoroughly and according to its own nature. Yes, it is not only opposed, but repulsive, invisibly and cruelly repulsive, something that takes my breath away, that drains the power from my muscles, that confuses my senses, stings me poisonously from behind in the heel, and always strikes just where I did not suspect I possessed a vulnerable spot.[207]

A new life emerges for Jung. His body is covered with green leaves and two figures reappear: the Red One who personifies joy[208], and Ammonius, the anchorite whom he had met in the desert during his solitude experience[209]. What is interesting here is that these figures arrive together and take Jung for Satan, since both had been influenced by him and for this reason experience what they had hitherto repressed. The anchorite surrendered to human company, drink, and women, and left for Italy. In Naples he met the Red One, who had imagined reforming the Church and introducing dance into the liturgy. At first he dances only before the altar, but then he cannot stop dancing, and dances in the mountains, in the desert, all the time. He finds his path again only in Naples, where he encounters Ammonius, who brings back his sanity.

Meeting with these images transforms Jung, placing him before what he himself had repressed. He writes:

> When I had seen death and all the terrible solemnity that is gathered around it, and had become ice and night myself, an angry life and impulse rose up in me. My thirst for the rushing water of the deepest knowledge began to clink with wine glasses; from afar I heard drunken laughter, laughing women and street noise. Dance music, / stamping and cheering poured forth from all over; and instead of the rose scented south wind, the reek of the human animal streamed over me. Luscious-lewd whores giggled and rustled along the walls, wine fumes and kitchen steam and the foolish cackling of the human crowd drew near in a cloud. Hot sticky tender hands reached out for me, and I was swaddled in the covers of a sickbed. I was born into life from below, and I grew up as heroes do, in hours rather than years. And after I had grown up, I found myself in the middle land, and saw that it was spring.[210]

It is interesting to note that the encounter between the Red One and Ammonius occurs in Naples. Jung had been to Naples in 1912, and in the dream from that year, on Christmas Eve, an Italian *loggia* appeared—as was already mentioned above. He attributed to this dream his decision to have a love relationship with Toni Wolff. The Latin culture, more extraverted, exuberant, and open to demonstrations of affection, and in this sense very different from the Swiss-German tradition, in which emotions remain more hidden, and people more serious, must have attracted Jung's attention, and for this reason served as the background to the encounter between the figures of his imagination.

We have an example of the distinction between Latin and German in the dialogue that Jung has with the Red One, on page 259 of the *Red Book*. In it, Jung says to the Red One, "it seems to me that you bring with you a strange air, something worldly, something impudent, or exuberant, or—in fact—something pagan," to which the Red One replies that Jung does not offend him, but that he wasn't an "old pagan." Jung then says, "I don't want to insist on that. You are also not pompous and Latin enough," thereby associating Latin with exuberant, mundane, pagan. Further along in this dialogue, Jung says, "I would before God always like to be as serious and true to myself as I try to be. However, that certainly becomes difficult in your presence. [...] you're bound to be from the black school of Salerno [...]." The Red One responds: "You're superstitious and too German."

The exuberance of the Latin world expressed by its light and its shadow—the world of luxury, prostitutes, drunks, full of music and laughter—makes Jung "a laughing being of the forest," "a forest goblin and prankster," "neither good nor bad, merely living," "utterly inconstant and superficial, and yet reaching deep down, down to the kernel of the world"[211].

Thus we see the transformation that Jung goes through after the experience with the dead and his opening up to a joyful life, symbolized by the integration of "his friends." "I had absorbed the life of both of my friends; a green tree grew from the ruins of the temple"[212]. He recognizes in himself the life of nature, a life that simply is, without any attributes, without moral judgment. It is the perception of life fructifying from Eros, represented by drunkenness and debauchery in the shadows, but brightly by joy and lightness. "After the cursing comes laughter, so that the soul is saved from the dead"[213].

In consequence of his elaboration of this experience, Jung realized that his ideals are no longer the same, which gives way to a new type of life—to his "greening tree."

It merits noting that according to Shamdasani[214] the illuminations on page 32 of the calligraphic volume that illustrate this chapter are similar to the mosaics of Ravenna. Jung had been there in 1913, returning in 1914 under special circumstances, as we will later see.

The New God

The path that leads Jung to his next adventure was hot and cold—one of his feet burned; the other froze. This was the beginning of the presence of opposites, a theme that Jung would elaborate throughout his work. He comes face to face with Izdubar, a hero who hoped to meet immortality in the West but is hurt by words coming from science and spoken by Jung. The perception that polarities are inside him and that it is impossible to change his nature, or to reject or to destroy that which belongs to him, increasingly penetrates his conscious, making him realize the antagonism in his soul. "It hurts, but you continue and look toward distant goals"[215].

Jung's emphasis on Logos, on reason, to the detriment of nature and the mythic dimension is noted, and he feels that he must not let the force of this other side, of this "God," represented by Izdubar, vanish. The result of this is the renewal of his God. Jung wrote about this:

> The renewed God signifies a regenerated attitude, a renewed possibility of life, a recovery of vitality, because, psychologically speaking, God always denotes the highest value, the maximum sum of libido, the fullest intensity of life, the optimum of psychological vitality.[216]

The transformation of his God points, therefore, in the direction of a recuperation of the intensity of life, possibly because Jung walked away from adapting to the "spirit of this time" toward the depth and meaning of his soul, discovering in her the presence of polarities. His new God embraces opposites, both with equal rights, both legitimate, and therefore both to be respected.

> He is the eternal emptiness and the eternal fullness.
> Nothing resembles him and he resembles everything.
> Eternal darkness and eternal brightness.
> Eternal below and eternal above.
> Double nature in one.
> Simple in the manifold.
> Meaning in absurdity.
> Freedom in bondage.
> Subjugated when victorious.
> Old in youth.
> Yes in no.[217]

Jung declares his love to this God, stressing that it was his love that transformed Him and gave Him the possibility of rebirth[218]. But, he adds, just as he gave birth to God, he animated the emptiness of matter from where evil grows[219].

We can address the issue of good and evil as the expression of conflict lived by Jung in his relationship with Toni Wolff and Emma Jung. In the imaginative process Jung met Izdubar, the God became weak, and Jung brought Him back to life. Although this occurred between 8—10 January 1914, the transcription in calligraphic script was completed only in February 1917[220]. Between the conclusion of the transcription and the description of the next vision (occurring on January 12, 1914), he inserted some paintings. Among them, there is the figure on page 71, in which three serpents are intertwined. It is probable that this is the image about which Jung said to Tina Keller: "See these three snakes that are intertwined. This is how we three struggle with this problem," referring to his relationship with Emma and Toni[221]. Regardless of whether this painting was originally produced in 1914, or later in 1917 (which is more probable, since the drawing on page 58 was made in January 1917), the fact is that these experiences associated with Izdubar led Jung to create this painting, making explicit the difficulty faced by the love triangle.

The perception of new meaning for his life is followed by his experience in the underworld. He feels that his incursion into this domain is fruit of the necessity to touch "the black bottom of human nature," so that it is possible to commune with God[222].

The experience that Jung later would identify with that of the Self (as central organizer of the psyche, that is, the Central Archetype) he described as the soul's splendor.

> From this you will understand that your God is alive and that your soul has begun wandering on remorseless paths. [...] Sometimes you no longer recognize yourself. [...] You want to set limits, but it compels you to keep going. [...] The fire burns right through you. That which guides forces you onto the way.[223]

But again he makes explicit the conflict that rages within him:

> But I'm ashamed of my God. [...] The divine appears to me as irrational craziness. I hate it as an absurd disturbance of my meaningful human activity. It seems an unbecoming sickness which has stolen into the regular course of my life. Yes, I even find the divine superfluous.[224]

At the same time that Jung perceives his internal fire, the splendor of his soul, and the path it points to, without remorse, he becomes ashamed of what he is living, feeling bad because his life is disturbed, believing even that the divine is "an irrational madness," "an inconvenient illness," and also "superfluous."

Divine Madness

There are countless passages we might interpret as due to Jung's conflict. In the visions of January 17, 1914, he elaborates the imitation of Christ, seeing in Him a model of someone capable of withstanding enormous suffering, symbolized by the cross that He bore, and also of transformation and new life. With Christ being a religious symbol of such magnitude, and His suffering an image of immeasurable pain, we can imagine what Jung felt to compare his suffering to that of Christ! The constant search for his essential truth, inspired by the example of the Messiah, brought him into conflict with his time:

> And so I am outside my time, despite the fact that my life is in this time and I am split between the life of Christ and my life that still belongs to this present time.[225]

The tension generated by these opposites was the same between thinking and feeling, desire and action:

> What thinking cannot solve, life solves, and what action never decides is reserved for thinking[226].

> So long as we live here on earth, we cannot escape temptation. [...] This knowledge had evidently brought me into conflict with society[227].

Jung then imagines being admitted to a hospice, and considers the "divine madness," "a higher form of the irrationality of the life streaming through us [...]"[228], but that could, in no way, be integrated into society of that time.

The divine madness, mentioned in retrospect by Jung at the beginning of the *Red Book*[229], is now experienced. In a footnote, Shamdasani amplifies this theme, referring to the Phaedrus by Plato. Madness, "provided it comes as a gift of heaven, is the channel by which we receive the greatest blessings"[230]. He reminds us that Socrates distinguishes between four types of divine madness: inspired guesswork, such as the prophetess at

Delphi; situations in which individuals prophesy and incite prayer and worship; possession by the Muses; and lover[231].

The divine madness is also Dionysian ecstasy and enthusiasm, which affected the maenads possessed by the god. The intensity of this experience does not allow it to be dominated by the ego, by willpower, and the person suffering from it knows/feels possessed by something that is beyond their ability to control. What makes this madness divine is the fact that the alteration of consciousness mobilized by deep emotions, sensuality, visceral experiences—and not just by reason—stimulates the experience of transcendence and produces a sense of wholeness and fullness. In Jung's words, "[...] there is a divine madness which is nothing other than the overpowering of the spirit of this time through the spirit of the depths"[232].

In the devotional Bhakti yoga cults from India, activities of play, emotional frenzy, and madness "signify that [the person] transcended the ordinary and participates in the extraordinary"[233]. Zimmer considers the sacred madness to come from ecstatic love[234]. Divine madness, in Jung's process, is the revelation of his feelings. "I enter the space of my feeling which was previously unknown to me"[235].

Joy and fear mingle. Initially, Jung asserted that Christianity of that time lacked the madness and therefore lacked divine life[236]. At that moment, he finds divine madness, and with it, Christ[237].

The Christ whom Jung rediscovers is the Gnostic Christ, the joyful Christ, who dances and loves, the Christ who suffers and is reborn to a new life, the Christ of alterity, not the institutionalized Christ, trapped in reductive patriarchal dogmas[238]. He continues:

> In this realm other laws are valid than the guidelines of my wisdom. Here, the "mercy of God," which I had never relied on, for good practical reasons, is the highest law of action. The "mercy of God" signifies a particular state of the soul in which I entrust myself to all neighbors with trembling and hesitation and with the mightiest outlay of hope that everything will work out well.[239]

Jung points out that Christ, the sacrificial victim to be devoured, reproduces customs of Antiquity, which here acquire another dimension, a different meaning, thanks to love. "In your sacred practice that which earlier laws condemned will once again be included"[240]. Saint Augustine said: "Love and do what you want."

The law of love, allowing one to assign a transcendent meaning even to the reprehensible, to transgression, admits accepting what was not accepted, and so Jung proposes that the dead—which appear in his visions, and he interprets as unfulfilled temptations and desires—are worthy of love. He considers that the temptation is the demand of those who died before their time to conform to the edicts of the law and good.

> What we call temptation is the demand of the dead who passed away prematurely and incomplete through the guilt of the good and of the law. For no good is so complete that it could not do injustice and break what should not be broken[241].

Jung recognizes that repression leads to premature death of that which could not exist without causing guilt. On the other hand, breaking the law and what is considered good may be necessary to what is essential—love, for example.

The feeling that emerges with all its intensity in Jung, as opposed to his most developed thinking, demands to be respected and revered. Love allows him to leave a position in which he believed he was in command of his life, for another in which he surrenders himself to the unknown or to the irrationality of life. It is this feeling that, if on one hand can lead him to chaos, on the other allows him to laugh and opens for him the door for the reunion with Christ. Thus, what has always existed and had no possibility of living should be reinstated under the law of love.

Jung feels the insecurity of one who is experiencing the unknown and foresees chaos. "This is the night in which all the dams broke, where what was previously solid moved, where the stones turned into serpents, and everything living froze"[242]. And he concludes that what is considered lower, inferior, can be saved from depravity through love.

Jung writes that the God of this time does not appear in flesh and does not live among men, as Christ, but is the son of man and appears in spirit, "born only through the spirit of the men conceiving the womb of the God"[243]. Shamdasani[244] draws attention to Jung's further elaboration in relation to this statement when he makes a comment about John's vision in Revelation and compares it to the writings of Meister Eckhart:

> This disturbing invasion engendered in him [John] the image of the divine consort, whose image lives in every man [...] It was he who knew that God alone in his Godhead is not in a state of bliss, but must be born in the human soul. The incarnation in Christ is the prototype which is continually being transferred to the creature by the Holy Ghost.[245]

This passage is remarkable because it allows us to consider that the disruption that took hold of Jung, also occurred due to the appearance of the "divine consort" that he would later call anima. This mobilization, probably originating from love, took the rug out from under him, shook his structure, and made him think he was mad. But he also accepted it as an expression of the Holy Spirit, which is experienced as God in us. The connection between love and transcendence, love and spirituality, love and fulfillment of the soul, love and his individuation process becomes even more explicit, making us feel the force this experience had over Jung. In fact, if love hadn't called to him so profoundly to fulfill his soul, perhaps he would not have ventured into such uncertain and unconventional terrain as to carry on his love relationship with two women simultaneously.

Jung reinforces the idea that "the God of this time will torment the spirit through the flesh," contrary to Christ who, "tormented the flesh through the spirit"[246]. Physical nature, which according to the law of the Father was overcome by the spirit, must now be reconsidered and find its place alongside the spirit through love.

The polarization between spirit and body creates a dichotomy that is seen as irreconcilable to patriarchal consciousness. Christ preached love and compassion, but the repressive institutionalization of His ideas directed this love mainly to the spirit, while the flesh was considered a source of sin. Jung, who had many Protestant ministers in his family, knew the patriarchal aspect of institutionalized Christianity intensely. He sought to insert into the symbol of Christ the matriarchal, carnal dimension, aiming to unite opposites as a search for wholeness. The realization of spirit into matter, the possibility of experiencing transcendence in body and in everyday life, was part of Jung's search. And this is what he found in alchemy.

It seems unnecessary to mention a still larger number of examples of the importance attributed by Jung to love and how he saw the inferior place conferred to it by collective consciousness, in comparison to the spirit and to Logos.

According to an Orphic cosmogony, at the beginning the goddess Night appeared as a black bird. But she did not come all alone, but with the Wind that fertilized her. She laid an egg from which was born a winged being: Eros, or as it was called later, Phanes, known as "firstborn shining one" and "he who reveals." Through this God, heaven and earth were created[247]. As the god of love, Eros brings with it the inherent possibility of synthesis, because, as stated by Plato in *The Symposium*, love is the desire and search for integration.

It is, therefore, significant that Shamdasani writes: "Phanes is Jung's God"[248].

Jung concludes that good and evil could only be evaluated in relation to development. If this happens, the opposites are united. And he adds that doubt is part of growth: the stronger person is able to admit it, while the weaker will be overwhelmed by it[249]. It describes Jung's process of individuation and his perception that good and evil are not good and bad in themselves, but depend on the context in which they are lived.

When the God [that is, love] came into his life, Jung accepted all that was reprehensible in himself, and thus paved the way for the action of God[250].

He recognizes that the inferior rests asleep like the dead and demands sacrifice, not of blood or milk, but of the will of the flesh[251].

The God who enters Jung's life is love, and it requires the awakening of dormant, repressed impulses, ones that are neither good nor bad but that could lead him to his development. Even though it seemed unworthy to him, these dead will be revered through the desire of the flesh, through sexuality, thus freeing "[...] the son of the earth, [...] the great suffering one, who needed salvation," "the most rejected"[252]. But for this to happen, the spirit, that is, Logos, must "lay dismembered on the altar"[253]. We must not forget that the early twentieth century was still marked by great repression of sexuality (especially for women) and feelings (especially for men). The body, the "son of the earth," was the great sufferer whom Jung seeks to praise and free when he assumes his love relationship with Toni, including her in his intimate, family, social and professional life.

The effect of this experience and this elaboration is described by Jung as follows and speaks for itself:

> The depths are silent. He has arisen and now beholds the light of the sun and is among the living. Restlessness and discord rose up with him, doubt and the fullness of life.
>
> Amen, it is finished. What was unreal is real, what was real is unreal. However, I may not, I do not want to, I cannot. Oh human wretchedness! Oh unwillingness in us! Oh doubt and despair. [...]
>
> Who succeeded in crossing the borders of this realm with good grounds, pure conscience, and obeying the law of love? [...] Who is it that descended from being one into being two? Who is it that tore apart his own heart to unite what has been separated?
>
> I am he [...] In that I accepted myself I divided myself into two, and in that I united myself with myself I became the smaller part of myself.[254]

The Way of the Cross

The cross points to the crucified, for whom living His own life demanded enormous sacrifice, who not only taught the knowable and that which deserved to be taught, but who lived it[255]. Undoubtedly, the main point of Jung's quest is to surpass the knowledge restricted to words or reason and to bring it to life, to experience, even if this means being crucified, since it implies confronting and elaborating what we feel to be most abject and despicable. Living one's own life, with all the difficulty that this implies, will be the center of his theory when he proposes that the goal of human life is the fulfillment of individuation.

Jung's struggle is reflected in his search for something that can guide him and that is neither will nor intention. He perceives that will and intention do not encompass his whole personality, and what he longs for is to experience totality, to be guided in his deepest process by his soul or by something that symbolizes his essence and that he would later theorize as Self (Central Archetype)[256]. It includes the possibility of embracing irrational, intuitive, illogical, and magical elements. He writes:

> The ancients devised magic to compel fate. They needed it to determine outer fate. We need it to determine inner fate and to find the way that we are unable to conceive.[257]

So, Jung decides to become an apprentice and search for a magician.

Philemon

January 27, 1914. On this day, in his imagination, Jung meets Philemon, the magician, who first expressed for him the symbol of the Wise Old Man.

But Philemon does not appear alone. Baucis, whom he married in his youth, accompanies him. In his book, *Metamorphosis*, Ovid tells the story of this destitute old couple who gave lodging in their home to Jupiter and Mercury. Disguised as poor people, the gods had been turned away by everyone else. The couple is offered a gift, and Philemon requests that for their prize he and Baucis be made priests to these gods, and that they die simultaneously, which is granted.

The initial encounter with Elijah is followed by Philemon's appearance, which indicates the transition of asceticism and isolation to someone who is confessedly a lover. If Elijah is the symbol of asceticism, Philemon symbolizes love. It is meaningful that the image that will point out the path to Jung is a symbol that joins love and spirituality. Jung considered the feeling of love a divine madness, which he contained and inserted into a spiritual and transcendent context.

Philemon and Baucis' life is simple, close to nature. "They water their bed of tulips and tell each other about the flowers that have newly appeared"[258]. Jung seeks out Philemon in search of magic, and learns that it is unknowable and incomprehensible[259]. Jung concludes that:

> A rational man of this time will therefore never use magic.
>
> But it is another thing for whoever has opened the chaos in himself. We

> need magic to be able to receive or invoke the messenger and the communication of the incomprehensible. We recognized that the world comprises reason and unreason; and we also understood that our way needs not only reason but also unreason. [...]
>
> [...] The magical way arises by itself. If one opens up chaos, magic also arises.
>
> [...] Magic is a way of living. If one has done one's best to steer the chariot, and one then notices that a greater other is actually steering it, then magical operation takes place. [...] But the condition is that one totally accepts it and does not reject it [...]
>
> [...]The uncertainty of such a life will most probably be its greatest burden, but still I must unite the two conflicting powers of my soul and keep them together in a true marriage until the end of my life, since the magician is called Philemon and his wife Baucis.[260]

Jung states that he unleashed the chaos within himself, reached beyond his rationality, which would have kept him from using magic. But what is magic? It is the mystery, the inexplicable, the irrational, the sacred. It is the emotion that awakens the soul, the transfiguration of the arid day to day. In this context, it is love.

And in an explicit way, Jung writes: "Thus I saw that the lover survives, and that he is the one who unwittingly grants hospitality to the Gods"[261]. That is, the gods take shelter where there is love. And he adds:

> Now I know your final mystery: you are a lover. You have succeeded in uniting what has been sundered, that is, binding together the Above and Below. [...] Why did I have to wander such long roads before I came to Philemon, if he was going to teach me what has been common knowledge for ages? Alas, we have known everything since time immemorial and yet we will never know it until it is has been accomplished. Who exhausts the mystery of love?[262]

The central theme of Jung's process in the *Red Book*—the encounter with love and his conflict in facing it—becomes ever more evident. After writing what is quoted above, he affirms: "You [Philemon] did not strike me as a lover. But my eyes were opened, and I saw that you are a lover of your soul [...]"[263].

And further on: "Your words left me to myself and my doubt"[264], and continuing: "Baucis is only your other half"[265], reducing the importance of the loved one in the life of the lover and denying the presence of the other person in Philemon's life, as though he lived completely alone!

Jung considers Philemon a master and friend of the dead, those who will become for Jung "the voices of the Unanswered, Unresolved, and Unredeemed"[266].

Philemon, the man capable of loving, was a symbol of extreme importance for Jung. He painted him in the *Red Book*, and by the side of the image wrote a phrase taken from the *Bhagavad Gita,* in which Krishna instructs Arjuna about the nature of truth: "Whenever there is a decline of the law and an increase in iniquity; then I put forth myself. For the rescue of the pious and for the destruction of the evildoers, for the establishment of the law I am born in every age" (chapter 4, verses 7 and 8).

The *Mahabharata*, one of the two great Hindu epics, is a poem fifteen times larger than the Bible. Its central theme is the great battle of Kurukshetra, waged between two groups of cousins disputing the succession of the kingdom. The central point of this work is the *Bhagavad Gita*, a sacred composition in the Hindu religion. In it, Arjuna, the hero of the battle, is instructed by the god Krishna, based on the laws of Dharma and Karma, to follow his profound truth, that which is and must be, even if this leads him to destroy part of his family[267].

Jung painted Philemon on a wall in one of the rooms of his tower in Bollingen, where he added the inscription: *Philemon sacrum, Fausti poenitentia* (Philemon's sanctuary, Faust's repentance). Is not the tower itself Jung's sanctuary, in which he conjugates Philemon's love and Faust's repentance and guilt?

Jung encounters a serpent, for whom he plays the flute and whom he calls soul and sister[268]. He considered the serpent a negative representation of the anima, contrary to the bird, whose image Jung saw as positive[269]. After his contact with Philemon, and the proximity with magic and love, Jung's anima makes herself present, and he perceives in the experience of paradoxes the path leading to his own soul. He recognizes that opposing polarities flow toward each other: sinful and holy, hot and cold, madness and reason, dark and light, and he experiences inside himself a savage battle till then unknown[270].

> How holy; how sinful, how everything hot and cold flows into one another! Madness and reason want to be married, the lamb and the wolf graze peacefully side by side. [...] My heart is filled with wild battle. The waves of dark and bright rivers rush together, one crashing over the other. I have never experienced this before.[271]

This is the expression of the conflict that Jung lived and which led him to write *The Transcendent Function* a few years later (in 1916), a text in which he affirms the need to bear a tension, a conflict, until "the last drop," for only then does the solution emerge through a symbol. As we have seen, and as Jung himself stated in his memoirs, the main concepts that he developed in his theory arose from the experiences of this period of his life. Thus, we can't ignore the magnitude of the conflict and suffering that he faced in this period, since he himself compares it to being crucified. He makes it explicit in his dialogue with the serpent:

> Jung: "[...] Loving reaches up to Heaven and resisting reaches just as high. They are entwined and will not let go of each other, since **the excessive tension seems to indicate the ultimate and highest possibility of feeling**." (emphasis mine)
>
> Serpent: "You express yourself emotionally and philosophically. You know that one can say all this much more simply. For example, one can say that you have fallen in love all the way from the worm up to Tristan and Isolde"[272].
>
> Jung: "Yes, I know, but nonetheless..."[273]

There it is. Jung knows he fell in love. He is no longer guided by thinking nor by his understanding; he forgot who he was and surrendered himself to his soul, getting a "painful joy" in return[274]. "You turn your pain into pleasure. You are twisted, blinded; just suffer, you fool," says the serpent, to which Jung responds: "This misfortune ought to make me happy"[275].

Elaborating this experience, he writes: "But wherever there is love, the serpentlike abides also. […] What is beyond the human that appears in love has the nature of the serpent and the bird […] Man stands in-between"[276].

In the *Seven Sermons to the Dead*, written by Jung in 1916, published in the *Red Book* as part of *Scrutinies* and also in *Memories, Dreams, Reflections*, we find this passage:

> The daimon of sexuality approaches our soul as a serpent. She is half human soul and is called thought-desire.
>
> The daimon of spirituality descends into our soul as the white bird. He is half human soul and is called desire-thought.[277]

This image illustrates well the association that Jung establishes between sexuality, the feminine and the serpent, and also between the spirit, the masculine, and the bird. Both bird and serpent belong to love, and Jung seeks to conciliate these two dimensions in his amorous experience—as he will later propose the integration of the anima in men and the animus in women.

Jung then has the experience of unifying opposites within himself, affirming that this did not happen from thinking but was created from the incandescent heat of the entrails—that is, from intense emotions[278]. In *The Psychology of the Transference*, written by Jung in 1946, he establishes a parallel between the images in the alchemical book *Rosarium Philosophorum* and the process of transference. In it, there is a passage referring to the intense and profound involvement of the alchemist with the alchemical process. About it, Jung says that often the alchemist does not know if it is he who is by the fire, mixing the substance, or if he is the substance being mixed[279]. This analogy denotes the high degree of emotion, inner mobilization, and even indiscrimination that possess the alchemist, and also the person in love.

> I have united with the serpent of the beyond. I have accepted everything beyond into myself. From this I have built my beginning. When this work was completed, I was pleased [...][280]

In this stage of the elaboration process, we feel that Jung has reached a certain stability, and that, for some time, he will enjoy the integration of opposites that he seems to have achieved. However, the next vision takes him to something very different, and even surprising, since the serpent, who lives in the depths and connects him to the beyond, to that which he is not conscious of or was repressed, encounters a hanged man. He appears before Jung and says that he had been condemned to be hanged for having poisoned and murdered his father, his mother, and his wife[281].

When I read this passage for the first time, still without realizing the importance of Jung's difficulties in the relationship with Toni Wolff, of the dramatic intensity of his love and his conflict, I asked myself why this man had to murder his wife. Considering that Jung had worked with Freud and suffered the influence of psychoanalysis, to kill one's parents could be seen as a relatively common symbol—to overcome the parental figures in order to break with one's identification with them and acquire ones own identity. But, the wife?! I then went to consult Jung's biographic data to see what was happening to him during that time. Before sharing with the reader the results of my research, I will return to Jung's vision.

The hanged man says that he killed them for the love of God, wanting his loved ones to arrive early in eternal bliss. Jung asked him about his interest in doing so, and he answered that he had better health than his wife, and that he wanted to live with his children. He believes he encounters his wife at times, after death, but that they talk only about trivial, impersonal things, as though they already had nothing to do with one another[282].

This impersonality is seen as a sort of Hell, which demonstrates the importance Jung gave to profound and significant relationships. The description of the relationship between the hanged man and his wife perhaps indicates the shadow of Jung's conjugal life—the distance between him and Emma. In an interview granted to Bair, Agathe, Jung's oldest daughter, "recalled with great emotion the happy times she and her husband spent lingering with their three children at the dinner table long after the meal was finished. She thought it sad that her own parents never knew such pleasure"[283].

In relation to Jung's home, Bair describes routine scenes that seem rather dispirited concerning the vibration of the conjugal relationship. Whenever Wolff knew that Jung would not have patients, she went to his house in the morning and stayed with him in the library, seated on the sofa, until the lunch hour. Jung walked to and fro, and they discussed, heatedly at times, ideas and impressions about his dreams and visions[284].

> […] Emma waited eagerly for the evening, when she could join her husband in his study. She sat on the same sofa that earlier bore Toni Wolff, reading in silence while he wrote or drew in the Black Books that he did not discuss with her. After several hours, she said good night just as quietly as she had sat and went off to her own bedroom at the far end of the house, leaving him still engrossed in self-scrutiny of one sort or another.[285]

In the sequence of the vision described above, the serpent says to Jung: "[…] you can never reconcile personal life with absolute life"[286], which indicates a glance at the impossibility of joining the full meaning of life, its essential and deep realization, with ordinary and daily life. Actually, this conjunction is the great challenge of individuation.

A little further along, Jung writes something that can be understood in relation to the hanged man's experience:

> While he feels as if a mysterious poison has paralyzed the living quality of his personal relations, the voices of the dead remain silent in his beyond; the threat, the fear, and the restlessness cease.[287]

In a footnote, Shamdasani transcribes one of Jung's observations from the margin of the calligraphic volume: "I still did not realize that I myself was this murderer"[288].

Jung says to the serpent that his work is done, to which she responds: "Nothing is accomplished yet. [...] This is only the beginning." And when Jung says that the dead are to be extinct, the serpent adds: "But then the living must first begin to live"[289].

We can infer from this passage that Jung admits his love ("A fool is one who exterminates his love for the sake of love,"[290]), and it calms him and silences the dead, but he recognizes that he still was not living love, and for this reason agrees with the serpent when she asks him if he did not feel empty[291]. I transcribe the dialogue between them:

Serpent: "Didn't you feel empty today? Do you call that life?"

Jung: "What you say is true, but I try to put as good a face as I can on everything and to settle for things."

Serpent: "That might be quite comfortable. But you really ought to make much higher demands."

Jung: "That I dread. I will certainly not assume that I could satisfy my own demands, but neither do I think that you are capable of satisfying them. [...]"[292]

The final dialogue brings the question of love to the surface. Jung believes he has completed his path, and the serpent/soul tells him that it is only beginning and that she would give him something in the form of an image. The vision of Elijah and Salome that follows is of extreme importance because it exposes, clearly and definitively, Jung's love problem. Salome is now cured of her blindness. She loves Jung, and Elijah gives her to him, and Jung asks what will he do with her, since he is married[293]. Jung admits now he also loves her. When Salome declares herself, and states she wants to live together with him, he feels crucified, and he says that the imperious need crucifies him and the impossibility cripples him. Now knowing the role of Toni Wolff in Jung's life, it is pertinent to think that this need that crucifies him occurs because it cannot be realized—at least, up until that moment. In note 324, on page 324, Jung alleges that this impossibility owes itself to the principles that came to him throughout his life as *insights*.

Mistrusting himself, he asks: "[...] what do you gain if one day I must lay you aside like a worn garment?"[294]. She feels ready to leave him, when his time comes. Jung responds:

> I know that it would be the greatest torment for me to let you go away. [...] I have not forgotten the dream where I saw my body lying on sharp needles and a bronze wheel rolling over my breast, crushing it. I must think of this dream whenever I think of love. If it must be, I am ready.[295]

This dream is depicted in the *Red Book,* page 127, under the name *Amore Triumphat* (Love Triumphs). Salome asks Jung to try, but he responds that to try is the same as to act, and this costs him greatly. "Just accept me," she says. He replies: "As if that would settle the matter! But being entangled with love! Simply thinking about it is dreadful"[296].

Jung then speaks to Salome about the importance of being complete and to relate based on that, and not on what one longs for. She does not have to be far from him, but he insists that Salome follow her own path, dancing, singing, and playing the lute for people.

Jung notes that he found pleasure in himself, and power over himself, while Salome lost pleasure, power of temptation, and learned love for the other, becoming herself love. If we understand Salome as an image of Jung's anima, we see that he is closer to overcoming the desire of pleasure and the power of seduction, and beginning to develop his capacity to love. However, at the same time, he is still unable to do it, although he desires it. He reveals having accepted Salome as pleasure, but rejected her as love, since he fears this feeling and cannot direct it to the world nor to people[297].

> I accepted Salome as pleasure, and reject her as love. [...] Love, I believe, belongs to others. But my love wants to be with me. I dread it. May the power of my thinking push it from me, into the world, into things, into men [...] I want to wage this battle to its end.[298]

This vision occurred on February 9, 1914. On the 11th, Jung continues, now talking with the serpent, which he calls soul in *Black Book* 4. Salome is crying, and Jung complains about the payment that the serpent has given him, because it demanded sacrifice. The serpent answers that life asks for sacrifice. Jung says that he rejected Salome and asks if this was not enough. "Too little for you," the serpent says. Jung asks if forcing his feeling to the background was not enough. The serpent says no, since this is easier than being further tortured by Salome. This is why she cries. Jung admits that he does not know what to do, saying he should rise above his own head, but he cannot do it. He then asks the serpent to question the beyond and seek advice in Heaven or in Hell[299].

It is easier for Jung to part from Salome, a symbol of love, than to face the challenge of loving her, since he is married. However, being faithful to his inner truth, he opens himself to a path that will be revealed, since he recognizes he is facing a situation he will not be able to solve only by thinking, or by using stereotyped solutions. He is living an intense moral crisis that he will later recognize as the trigger of his individuation process. In this process, Jung shows the disposition to follow what he will propose theoretically: fidelity and submission of the ego to the Self, the recognition of the Self as something greater, the opening to the transcendent function, the quest for wholeness and individuation, for the ultimate realization of being. There is no doubt that, concerning living what he taught, Jung was an example.

The serpent transforms itself into a white bird that flies to Heaven, going beyond the clouds. The white bird asks Jung if he can hear it, and says that it found something for him, a golden crown. "And now it already lies ..."[300]. It is precisely here that Jung interrupts the calligraphic volume of the *Red Book*. We would not be Jungians if we did not ask ourselves what symbol is contained in the exact point in which Jung stops transcribing his experiences, and its meaning.

The very moment when the serpent, the chthonic representation of the anima—including here sexuality—transforms into the white bird, a more spiritualized representation of the anima, is a turning point. The anima reveals herself to be the carrier of something celestial, of a transcendent love that can unveil wholeness. The undeveloped feeling function, which identified her with pleasure, was transformed. Without doubt it became more difficult to repudiate, repress, or deny this experience from this point onward. No matter how strong one's preconceived ideas, they will not be able to restrain the power of love urging for totality.

Henceforth, Jung's visions transcribed by the editor of the *Red Book* were taken from the draft. The passage interrupted continues: "And now it already lies in my hand, a golden royal crown," on which is engraved: "Love never ends"[301]. This phrase, from Corinthians 1, 13:8, was so important for Jung that he repeats it in his *Memories*[302]. In the Bible, the phrase is inserted in a chapter entitled "Love is the supreme gift of all."

In his imagination, Jung was hanging from the branches of the divine tree for three days and three nights—a metaphor for the situation of conflict, from which we cannot escape without mutilating part of our personality. What we can do in this circumstance is wait. And that is what he does, waiting for help from "above." The crown was felt simultaneously as "the crown of eternal life," and "the crown of martyrdom"[303]. Is this not the paradox of "impossible" love?

Jung hangs between Heaven and Earth, and he fears to remain there forever, because "love never ends". Love can be considered the path toward the unification of opposites and, thus, Salome is represented as part of Jung: "Salome is what you are. Fly, and she will grow wings"[304]. Softly, Jung slips from the top of the tree to earth.

In his elaboration on these experiences, Jung writes: "As long as love goes pregnant with life, it should be respected; [...]"[305]. But his conflict is terrible: "Why; Oh spirit of the darkest depths, do you force me to say that whoever loves does not live and whoever lives does not love? I always get it backward!"[306].

We can understand his conflict between life and love symbolizing respectively the antagonism between the spirit of this time and the spirit of the depths, between life inside the moral collective and love with its transgressions. Jung attacks the spirit of the depths, because it revealed his contradictions: "You broke love and life in twain"[307].

Jung feels the product of his soul, the result of his process, to be a son of darkness, son of the demon, which weakens him. He identifies him, in a moment of hate, with Philemon, he who loves, by whom Jung feels deceived.

Further along, we read: "Where is Salome? Where is the unresolvable question of love? No more questions, my gaze is turned to the coming things, and Salome is where I am"[308]. After so much struggle and tension, it seems that a certain peace emerges. Salome, the anima, is perceived as inseparable from Jung. She is also a symbol of Eros, of the principle of relatedness, which Jung needed to learn how to coexist.

The *Black Book* 4 contains a fable told to Jung by the serpent (soul). In summary, it tells the following: a king could not have children. So he goes to a sorceress and has a child with her help. When the child grows up and covets the throne, the king goes back to the sorceress and she causes the death of his son. In deep sorrow, the king goes back to her, and she teaches him what to do to have another child. When this second son grows up and wants the throne, the king becomes intensely moved and gives him his crown. Jung will talk with the serpent about this fable and she tells him that he is this son, and so Jung should remain a child. We can understand this son, symbolically, as the dawn of a new consciousness against which Jung had rebelled. This new consciousness is capable of enduring the tension between the opposites. Jung writes, at the end of this passage: "My love remained with me"[309]. This was written on February 23, 1914.

The next annotation was made on April 19 of the same year. These dates are very important, because between March 30 and April 13, 1914, according to Shamdasani, Jung went on holiday to Italy. Bair[310] enters into more detail and states that during this period, just two weeks after Emma gave birth to their fifth daughter, Emma Helene, on March 18, Jung went to Ravenna with Toni Wolff. Emma and the baby remained under the care of Jung's mother-in-law, while the older children stayed with his mother.

Bair adds that Ravenna came to have special significance for Jung, as we can see in *Memories*, in which Jung describes going to Ravenna years later, accompanied by a lady—Bair affirms that it was Wolff[311]. In the Orthodox Baptistery, both shared a vision for some twenty minutes. They saw four mosaic frescoes. Afterward, they discovered that these no longer existed. We realize the degree of psychic intimacy and symbiosis that existed between them, that they could have the same vision at the same time. "This experience in Ravenna is among the most curious events in my life," says Jung[312]. And further on, he writes: "In the course of my confrontation with the anima I had actually had a brush with those perils which I saw represented in the mosaics. I had come close to drowning"[313].

With these objective facts at hand, the drama lived by Jung becomes even clearer. Were he not so touched by the anima, so mobilized by love, probably he would not have included Wolff in his social life. On reading the *Red Book*—and this is confirmed by Jung himself in *Appendix* B[314]—we see that the central process developed in it is the presence and the elaboration of the anima and of the principle of Eros. Well, hardly the rupture from Freud or even the First World War would mobilize a process like this. Even though these situations had, in some way, contributed to the visions described in the *Red Book*, any experienced analyst would agree that they can in no way be considered central to unleashing the development of Eros, of the feeling function, of the love relationship, and of the anima.

A member of the Swiss bourgeoisie, married to the heiress of the second largest fortune in the country, developing a brilliant and internationally renowned career, his wife pregnant for the fifth time, falling in love with another woman provoked enormous turbulence in Jung's life. Due to his permanent interest in observing his inner world, considering it important and deserving great respect, he would not be satisfied to choose one side of the conflict, in order to solve it rationally. His personality demanded that he remain at the crossroads until the end, until something greater than his will occurred. The discovery of the transcendent function did not happen without tremendous suffering.

After the trip to Ravenna, Jung returns to his annotations in the *Black Books*. In *Scrutinies*[315], written on April 19, 20 and 21, 1914, he comes upon his I and, in a monologue, lets go and casts his hate, his frustration, and his indignation upon his other I. Possibly mobilized by guilt, he expresses his desperation, and openly attacks his inner "other," projecting on him characteristics of the shadow and openly repudiating him, calling him barbarian, and promising to make his life a living hell, until he transforms into someone he can bear to live with[316].

> My I, you are a barbarian. I want to live with you, therefore I will carry you through an utterly medieval Hell, until you are capable of making living with you bearable.[317]

A confrontation with the shadow occurs here. Almost all of Jung's speech revolves around his repudiation of this I, mistreating and expressing his displeasure with him. Jung treats him as a liar, a coward, dishonest, poisonous, vengeful, possessing childlike pride, shameless, ambitious, thirsty for fame, and so on, adding that he is patient only in relation to its pleasure, having had minuscule progress since the Middle Ages[318].

> Only when it concerns your pleasure do you praise your patience. [...]
>
> [...] I will increase this pleasure until you vomit with joy so that you know what taking pleasure in self-torment means.
>
> [...] I will break your bones until there is no longer a trace of hardness there.
>
> [...] Your progress since the early Middle Ages appears to be minuscule.[319]

Jung also writes that if this other were not himself he would already have cut it to pieces[320].

After his trip with Wolff, in the already mentioned circumstances, it is not surprising that Jung exacerbates his self-criticism. Knowing what was happening in his external life, we can imagine the state of his emotions, and perceive the guilt and remorse he feels for having left his wife and a two-week-old daughter to take a honeymoon with his lover. His shadow that he called "my I," "stupid brother" in this passage, led him through the heart's path, i.e., through his less developed function. He used to say, when he spoke about his adulterous behavior in this period: "Back then I was in the midst of the anima problem"[321].

On April 20, 1914, Jung renounced the presidency of the International Psychoanalytic Association. He was in full confrontation with the shadow. Although he was slowly beginning to be able to be alone with himself, he often relapsed, became anxious, and another clash followed[322].

> After I had spoken these and many more angry words to my I, I noticed that I began to bear being alone with myself. But the touchiness still stirred in me frequently and I had to lash myself just as often.[323]

On April 30, 1914, Jung renounced his position as professor in the Faculty of Medicine at the University of Zurich.

In the month of May, Jung reencounters his soul. He and "his I" are suffering immersed in the hot embers left by the fire that he experienced so deeply[324]. His soul was happy and felt satisfied with what torments him—the experience of love nourishes the wings of the soul, but lacerates the heart immersed in guilt.

The soul says to Jung that he doubts, due to his weakness and disbelief, and not for love of men. "Stay on your way and do not run away from yourself. There is a divine and a human intention"[325]. She adds that sacrifice is necessary, and Jung says that he fears committing an injustice to men if he follows his path. His sadness continues. On June 24, 1914, his soul speaks to him again: "The greatest comes to the smallest," and nothing more was said.

At the beginning and end of June, and again at the beginning of July 1914, Jung had three very similar dreams.

> [...] I was in a foreign land, and suddenly, overnight and right in the middle of summer, a terrible cold descended from space. All seas and rivers were locked in ice, every green living thing had frozen.[326]

The second dream was thoroughly similar to this. But the third dream at the beginning of July went as follows:

> I was in a remote English land. It was necessary that I return to my homeland with a fast ship as speedily as possible. I reached home quickly. In my homeland I found that in the middle of summer a terrible cold had fallen from space, which had turned every living thing into ice. There stood a leaf-bearing but fruitless tree, whose leaves had turned into sweet grapes full of healing juice through the working of the frost. I picked some grapes and gave them to a great waiting throng.[327]

The interpretation that Jung gives to these dreams is associated with war—the cold of death, the sterile tree whose leaves have been transformed by the cold into medicine and whose fruits he gives to the multitude in the form of an intoxicating, bitter-sweet drink, that will leave a taste of blood in the mouth[328].

However, this is not the only possible interpretation. After having traveled with Wolff to another country, Jung encounters a terrible cold in his native country, in his house, in his home—it is not difficult to imagine how Jung found Emma, still in the puerperium, when he returned home. He was "in full summer"—again, the metaphor of heat—but it was impossible for him to avoid an uncommon cold. After the trip that Jung and Wolff took to Ravenna, Emma, who until then always welcomed her mother and sister to her home, restricted their visits to avoid embarrassment, since Wolff became a constant presence in her home[329].

When, in 1944, Jung suffers a heart attack and becomes very ill, Emma begins to control his visitors and, thus, Wolff is barely allowed to see him at this time—which shows that, thirty years later, Emma still resented her presence and, only then, during Jung's severe illness, was she able to impose her will.

But, let us return to the dreams. During the temporary withholding of life, when vegetation takes cover awaiting spring, a tree produces fruits—sweet grapes, which will originate a healing beverage.

Since these images come from a dream, once again I am impressed by the capacity of the organizing center of our psyche, the Self, to create such meaningful symbols. In principle, any fruit can be produced, but Jung himself taught that an oneiric symbol is never fortuitous. An apple is an apple, and cannot be substituted in our interpretation by any other fruit, since there would be no reason for a dream not to express the best possible image for what it wishes to convey.

Thus, grapes are grapes. And, not by chance, they have a special place in two great myths: that of Dionysos and that of Christ. The grape is the *prima materia* of wine, the central drink in the Dionysian initiation rites, since they produce an alteration of consciousness. In the Christian myth, wine represents the blood of Christ, consecrated in the altar. Jesus said:

> Truly, truly, I say to you, unless you eat the flesh of the Son of Man and drink His blood, you have no life in yourselves. He who eats My flesh and drinks My blood has eternal life, and I will raise him up on the last day (John 6: 53.54).

Both myths express sacrifice, death, and rebirth. And it is precisely to sacrifice, death, and rebirth that the oneiric images point. He passed from a "frozen" state, without emotions and apparent death, to the possibility of a new life that would even be disseminated through his theory. This transformation could only be achieved because Jung allowed himself to live his drama deeply.

The War

> And then the War broke out. This opened my eyes about what I had experienced before, and it also gave me the courage to say all of that which I have written in the earlier part of this book.[330]

On referring to the eruption of the war and attributing to it what he had written up till then, providing an extraordinary example of his privileged intuition, Jung minimizes, not to say excludes, his private experiences, which he had hitherto believed to be fundamental to his process. He affirms that he always wanted to understand his dialogue with the soul in relation to himself[331].

We can imagine the emotional impact of a war, especially a war of the magnitude of the First World War, unseen until then. For someone of Jung's sensibility, this situation must have touched him deeply, as demonstrated by his vision of the map of Europe covered with blood.

The submission of the spirit of the depths to the spirit of this time, an experience Jung seeks to shake off throughout the *Red Book*, creates such an imbalance in collectivity that it provokes wars. These nowadays—as in Jung's time—have as root the desire for power and control, economic interests, submission of one people by another, authoritarianism. War always produces disregard for the soul, for humanity, for nature, the absence of compassion, the impossibility of placing oneself in the other's position, neglecting the principle of Eros.

Before the War broke out, Jung lived his personal "war" with great suffering, anguish, tension, revolt, conflict, hate, love, despair, and guilt. It is worthy to observe that the dialogue between Jung and his soul, written on May 24, 1914, in which he speaks about his fear of committing an injustice to humankind, and hears that he should follow his path without worrying about others, whether they be good or bad[332], reminds us of the dialogue between Krishna and Arjuna, in the *Bhagavad Gita*, and the advice Krishna gives to the warrior.

It is not by chance that, at the image of Philemon's side[333], Jung transcribes a dialogue between Krishna and Arjuna, taken from the *Bhaga-*

vad Gita, in which the god Krishna incites the hero Arjuna to fight his cousins, his uncle, and his preceptor, that is, he is urged to participate in the destruction of his family.

Jung was relieved at the war's outbreak, since he feared he was becoming schizophrenic. In a letter to Mircea Eliade, he writes:

> On July 31st, immediately after my lecture [in Aberdeen], I learned from the newspapers that war had broken out. Finally I understood. And when I disembarked in Holland on the next day; nobody was happier than I. Now I was sure that no schizophrenia was threatening me.[334]

Involved with Toni Wolff, Jung repeated in a certain way the extramarital relation he had with Sabina Spielrein. The conflict generated by this situation, by his feeling of love and guilt—and almost revolt—was possibly so intense that the tension and suffering that he experienced were compared to the devastation caused by schizophrenia. Faced with the threat of losing his sanity, the war seemed a relief to him.

Thus, I believe that when Jung states that the war opened his eyes to what he was experiencing and gave him the courage to share it in the *Red Book*, actually he encounters a comfortable and politically correct explanation to maintain his *persona*. Thus he could reveal the extraordinary depth and creativity of his process, and at the same time hide the true importance of his relationship with Wolff.

After these experiences, the voices of the depths went silent for a year[335]. It was during this period that Jung began to make the calligraphic copy of *Liber Novus* from the *Black Books*, inserting the images in the *Red Book*, as well as adding some observations.

As we know, his process continued after this year and lasted his whole life. But the most meaningful experience underlying the *Red Book* occurred between 1913-1914, and cannot be separated from the time when Jung began his love relationship with Wolff.

Until the beginning of 1914, Wolff was the only person to read the *Black Books*. Bair[336] believes that Jung only permitted Emma to read some passages of his annotations in 1915—i.e., after the First World War had begun. Hannah affirms that during the first stages of the "confrontation with the unconscious," the positive aspect of Jung's anima was extensively projected onto Wolff[337].

The simultaneous relationship with Emma and Toni Wolff could never have been easy to manage. Jung insisted on treating the two equally, telling Emma that "he could not treat Wolff as anything less respectful than 'his other wife' "[338]. Thus, both related socially with each other, were members of the Psychological Club, wrote about themes concerning analytic psychology, and treated patients.

Jung and Wolff distanced themselves from each other when he became interested in alchemy and she did not. At this time, he also stopped copying the *Red Book.* "All of a sudden Toni Wolff went out of my life just as fast as she came in. All of a sudden, that was the end"[339]. Was it synchronicity that Jung interrupted the *Red Book* when he distanced himself from Toni Wolff? However, in fact, this distancing was never complete.

At the end of the 1940s, a "gracious and generous accommodation" developed between Toni Wolff and Emma, and lasted until Wolff's death on March 21, 1953[340]. Emma died on November 30, 1955.

Jung's testimony in *Memories, Dreams, Reflections* is meaningful:

> After my wife's death in 1955, I felt an inner obligation to become what I myself am. To put it in the language of the Bollingen house, I suddenly realized that the small central section which crouched so low, so hidden, was myself! [...] So, in that same year, I added an upper story to this section, which represents myself, or my ego-personality. Earlier, I would not have been able to do this; I would have regarded it as presumptuous self-emphasis. Now it signified an extension of consciousness achieved in old age. With that the building was complete.[341]

After Wolff's and Emma's deaths, Jung realizes the meaning of the tower, considering that the central part imprisoned between the two towers was himself—placed, we can imagine, between Emma and Toni. He felt that it was time to raise this building, permitting him to be taller than the sides in the same way he surpassed both women in longevity.

As a tribute to both women, and expressing their meaning in Jung's life, he carved into stones "the foundation of this house", referring to Emma; and "the fragrance of this house", dedicated to Toni Wolff[342].

FINAL CONSIDERATIONS

What occurs between the lover and the beloved
is the entire fullness of the Godhead[343].

There is no doubt that Jung contributed much to the idea that his process in the *Red Book* was due to his rupture with Freud or even to his premonition about the First World War. However, in Appendix B, on page 365 of the *Red Book*, we can read an interpretation, taken from the draft, that Jung makes of his own process through the images of Elijah and Salome. He writes about typological *enantiodromia*, in his case, the development of the feeling function rather than thinking. Jung refers to the development of the Eros and Logos polarity, which he understood as the principle of relatedness and of logic, respectively. Extensively developed in his theory, the principle of Eros manifests itself spontaneously in the course of his visions, generating intense emotional reactions and leading him to recognize elements of his soul that previously went unnoticed. He reveals, thus, that the search for the development of the capacity to love is a central point in his individuation process.

In an interview with Miguel Serrano dated May 1959, Jung said that nothing was possible without love, because only the person in love puts the entire personality in play and even risks life, allowing himself, at almost eighty-four years of age, to wonder:

> In some place, some time, there was a Flower, a Stone, a Crystal; a Queen, a King, a Palace; a Lover and his Beloved, a long time ago, in the Sea, an island, five thousand years ago… It is love, it is the Mystic Flower of the Soul, it is the Center, it is the Self… […] No one understands this, if not some poets, only they will understand me…[344]

I ask myself if the lack of vision of the Jungian community relative to the importance of love in Jung's life does not reflect the cultural devaluation of feeling and love in the life of men. How could Jung, a genius, a scholar, a creative man, be so affected by Eros' arrows to the point of believing that he was going mad? How could a profound thinker, dedicated to his work, allow himself to be so tormented by a woman? But isn't this exactly what he taught us by describing the effects of possession by the anima?

To see Jung with his conflicts, in the midst of his difficulties, pains, contradictions, and defenses, does not diminish him. To the contrary, it adds still more humanity to his image.

If there is something that we can affirm with certainty it is that Jung wrote what he lived and, in this sense, knew what he said. Perhaps for this reason his theory is spreading increasingly throughout the world, each one of us feeling and intuiting the deep truth of the words of someone who experienced them.

I believe that the best way to close this book is to give, once again, the word to Jung and let him speak about his experience with love.

> In my medical experience as well as in my own life I have again and again been faced with the mystery of love, and have never been able to explain what it is. [...] here is the greatest and smallest, the remotest and nearest, the highest and lowest, and we cannot discuss one side of it without also discussing the other. No language is adequate to this paradox. [...] "Love ceases not" [...]. Man can try to name love, showering upon it all the names at his command, and still he will involve himself in endless self-deception. If he possesses a grain of wisdom, he will lay down his arms and name the unknown by the more unknown, *ignotum per ignotius*—that is, by the name of God. That is a confession of his subjection, his imperfection, and his dependence; but at the same time a testimony to his freedom to choose between truth and error.[345]

GLOSSARY

Alterity Archetype—a concept proposed by Carlos Byington to describe an archetypal pattern of consciousness. It facilitates a dialectical relationship and a lack of hierarchy between the polarities. It is the archetype of paradox and metaphor. It is expressed in democracy, solidarity, compassion, and in everything in which a symmetric function exists.

Anima—According to Jung, the anima is an archetype present in men and represents the image of the feminine. Today, anima is considered the function that permits men to relate to the Other in dialectic circumstances. It can be expressed through a person, an object, a career, a work of art, a religious, political or vocational calling, that is, in all that constellates men's soul in search of totality. Anima is the propelling motive (psychopomp) for the process of individuation of men beginning in adolescence and continuing mainly in the second half of life.

Animus—An archetype present in women, equivalent to the anima in men. It permits women to relate to the Other in a dialectic way. Animus is the archetype responsible for mobilizing the spirit of a woman (psychopomp), impelling her to follow her calling to fully develop her personality.

Archetype—Universal possibility for expressing one's nature. It is present in everyone. Being virtual, we only have access to its individual or collective manifestations, as, for instance, in dreams, images, myths, religions, fairy tales, physical and mental symptoms, relationships, and in all human experiences. An archetype only manifests itself if it is activated (constellated). Everything is archetypal, since nothing we experience is alien to human nature.

Central Archetype—The principal archetype, so-called only once by Jung in his work (*Symbols of Transformation*, CW 5, par. 497). Carlos Byington utilizes this terminology to refer to the organizing center for the development of the personality, i.e., the Self.

Enantiodromia—Pendular movement of the psyche, which leads unilateral parts of the personality to go from one extreme to the other. The more the functioning of a person is unilateral, the more intense *enantiodromia* will be. For example, the moralist who transforms in debauchery, or the workaholic who abandons work and goes on to cultivate his idleness.

Eros—The principle of emotional relationship with people, animals, nature, and things.

Feeling Function—The reason of the heart. It is a rational function associated with ethical judgment, evaluating what is right or wrong, good or bad etc.

Individuation—Instinct or drive toward self-realization. An impulse to actualize the personality's full potential in order to develop consciousness and integrate polarities. Individuation does not mean individualism, since it implies considering oneself just as important as the other.

Intuitive Function—Leads people to understand internal or external aspects, without there being a logical or sensorial path to this. It is an irrational function that permits one to foresee the future or to dive into the unknown past.

Jungian Typology—Jung classified four functions of consciousness, two rational (feeling and thinking), and two irrational (intuition and sensation). An attitude of introversion or extraversion is associated with each of these functions, resulting in eight types: introverted sensation, extraverted sensation, introverted intuition, extraverted intuition, introverted feeling, extraverted feeling, introverted thinking, and extraverted thinking.

Logos—Logical, abstract function. It permits the individual to have objectivity, distance and impersonality.

Matriarchal Archetype—Utilized here in accordance with a concept proposed by Byington, it refers to the functioning of consciousness guided by sensuality, intimacy, spontaneity, pleasure, and attentiveness to its own rhythm and to its own needs. The polarities function here in an insular way and, for this reason, the matriarchal archetype favors symbiosis. This archetype is present in man, in woman, and in culture.

Numinous—That which possesses *numen*, an expression used by Rudolf Otto to express the experience of the sacred, which he characterized as an experience of *tremendum et fascinosum*.

Patriarchal Archetype—Is herein understood in accordance with the Jungian Symbolic Psychology of Carlos Byington. It is a pattern of functioning consciousness in man, in woman and in culture, in which the polarities act in a polarized and hierarchical manner. It is the archetype of organization, or rule and of law.

Persona—The archetype responsible for the individual's social presentation. The more secure the person is, the more flexible and multi-faceted its persona will be. It is expressed in gestures, voice, fashion and behavior, as well as through professions and roles we play, for instance the role of mother, father, son, teacher, doctor, politician etc.

Self—Jung utilizes this term in two distinct senses. One of them refers to the totality of the psyche, and the other to the principal of archetypes, which is the organizing center of personality.

Sensation Function—An irrational function, Jung called it the reality function. It tells us what something is. It enables the individual to deal with the minutia of internal and external realities in a pragmatic way.

Shadow—Jung considered this the undesired, unconscious aspect of the personality. The shadow has contents that are difficult to integrate into consciousness. The integration of these contents is indispensable to personality's plenitude.

Synchronicity—The significant coincidence between subjective and objective events. For instance, the relationship between dreams and fantasies and occurrences in the external world without a causal connection. Jung considered synchronicity to be an acausal principle of relationship.

Syntonic—Aligned, in tune with.

Thinking Function—A rational function that permits one to articulate logically and abstractly ideas, emotions, images and perceptions of inner and outer reality.

Transcendent Function—Central function of symbolization. It manifests when the tension between opposites is held in consciousness.

NOTES

1. Jung, C. G. the *Red Book*, p. 301, note 211.

2. Ibid., p. 237, note 81.

3. Jung, C. G. *Memories, Dreams, Reflections*, p. 199.

4. This book was compiled by Aniela Jaffé between 1957 and 1959, but in some instances it was written by Jung in his own hand, which adds a quality of autobiography.

5. Jung, *Red Book*, p. 367.

6. Ibid., p. 336.

7. Shamdasani, Sonu. Introduction to *Red Book*.

8. Ibid., p. 210.

9. Ibid., p. 220.

10. Jung, *Red Book*, p. 200, note 70.

11. Shamdasani, Introduction to *Red Book*, p. 221.

12. Ibid., p. 220.

13. Jung, C. G. *The Visions Seminars,* Book 1, p. 2.

14. Hannah, Barbara. *Jung: His Life and Work. A Biographical Memoir.*

15. Bair, Deirdre. *Jung: A Biography.*

16. Ibid., p. 208.

17. Hannah, *Jung.*

18. Jung, *Analytical Psychology: Notes on the Seminar Given in 1925*, p. 112.

19. Emma, born Rauschenbach, married Jung in 1903.

20. McGuire, William, ed., *The Freud/Jung Letters: The Correspondence Between Sigmund Freud and C. G. Jung*, p. 243.

21. Ibid., p. 247.

22. Ibid., pp. 247f.

23. Ibid., pp. 244f.

24. Jung, *Memories,* pp. 163ff.

25. Ibid., pp. 163f.

26. Jung, *Analytical Psychology*, p. 39.

27. Jung, *Memories,* p. 165.

28. Byington, Carlos. *Jungian Symbolic Psychology.*

29. Jung, *Memories,* p. 165.

30. Barros, José D'A. "Os trovadores medievais e o amor cortês—reflexões historiográficas." *Revista Aletheia—Estudos sobe Antiguidade e Medievo*, p. 5.

31. Jung, *Red Book*, p. 366.

32. Barros, José D'A. "Os trovadores, pp. 5f.
33. Pronounced by a "court of love" in 1174. Rougemont, in Barros, p. 9.
34. Ibid., p. 7.
35. Ibid., p. 9.
36. Ibid., p. 6.
37. Ibid., p. 14.
38. Jung, *Memories,* pp. 171f.
39. Jung, *The Psychological Aspects of the Kore*, CW 9i, par. 371.
40. Jung, *The Psychology of the Transference*, CW 16, par. 380.
41. Carotenuto, Aldo. *A Secret Symmetry—Sabina Spielrein Between Jung and Freud.*
42. Psychiatric hospital where Jung began to work once he graduated, in 1900.
43. Carotenuto, *Secret Symmetry,* p.144.
44. Ibid., p.161.
45. Ibid., p.166.
46. Ibid., p.167.
47. Ibid., pp.168f.
48. McGuire, *Freud/Jung Letters,* p. 139.
49. Shamdasani, Introduction to *Red Book*, p. 198.
50. Ibid., p. 214.
51. Ibid., pp. 204f.
52. Ibid.
53. Jung, *Memories,* p. 188.
54. Jung, *Red Book*, p. 238.
55. Ibid., p. 229.
56. Ibid.
57. Ibid.
58. Ibid.
59. Ibid., p. 230.
60. Ibid.
61. Ibid., p. 178.
62. Jung, *Memories,* p. 175.
63. Ibid., p. 175.
64. Bair, *Jung.*
65. Ibid., p. 727, note 10.
66. Jung, *Analytical Psychology*, p. 43.

67. Ibid., p. 248.

68. Jones, in ibid., p. 206.

69. Bair, *Jung*, p. 241.

70. Ibid., p. 249.

71. Ibid., p. 730, note 39.

72. Jung, *Red Book*, p. 231.

73. Jung, *Aion—Researches into the Phenomenology of the Self.* CW 9ii.

74. Jung, *Red Book*, pp. 231f.

75. Ibid., p. 232.

76. Ibid.

77. Ibid., p. 233, note 48.

78. Ibid., p. 232.

79. Jung, *Visions Seminars.* Book 1, p. 5.

80. Jung, *Psychological Commentary on Kundalini Yoga*, p. 45.

81. Guerra, Maria Helena R. M. "Encontro: O Relacionamento Interpessoal Dialético enquanto Símbolo de Totalidade", p. 15.

82. Jung, *Red Book*, p. 233.

83. Ibid., note 49.

84. Ibid., p. 233.

85. This monologue is reprinted from Goethe, W., *Faust.*

86. Jung, *Red Book*, p. 234.

87. Ibid.

88. Ibid., p. 235.

89. Jung, *Memories,* p. 191.

90. Jung, *Red Book*, pp. 235f.

91. Ibid., p. 236.

92. Ibid.

93. Ibid.

94. De, S. K. *Early History of the Vaisnava Faith and Movement in Bengal.*

95. Guggenbühl-Craig, Adolph. *Marriage—Dead or Alive?* p. 85.

96. Jung, *Red Book*, p. 236.

97. Ibid.

98. Ibid.

99. Ibid.

100. Ibid., p. 237.

101. Ibid.

102. Jung, *Analytical Psychology*, p. 48.

103. Jung, *Red Book*, p. 239.
104. Jung, *Analytical Psychology*, p. 50.
105. Ibid.
106. Kerényi, Karl. *Dionysos—Archetypal Image of Indestructible Life*, p. 61.
107. Ibid., pp. 224f.
108. Ibid., p. 279.
109. Shamdasani, Introduction to *Red Book*, p. 237, note 83.
110. Brandão, Junito de S. *Mitologia Grega*, vol. 1.
111. Ibid., vol. 2, p. 132.
112. Ibid.
113. Jung, *Red Book*, p. 238.
114. Ibid.
115. Jung, *Analytical Psychology,* p. 92.
116. Ibid., p. 94.
117. Jung, *Red Book*, p. 238.
118. Guerra, Maria Helena R. M. "Encontro."
119. Jung, *Red Book*, p. 239, note 92.
120. Ibid., p. 239.
121. Jung refers to this material as a dream in *Memories,* and as a vision in the *Red Book.*
122. Jung, *Red Book*, pp. 241-242.
123. Jung, *Memories,* p. 180.
124. Jung, *Analytical Psychology*, p. 57.
125. Jung, *Red Book*, p. 242, note 115.
126. Ibid., p. 242.
127. Jung, *Analytical Psychology*, p. 56.
128. Ibid., p. 57.
129. Jung, *Memories,* pp. 180f.
130. Jung, *Red Book*, p. 245.
131. Bair, *Jung,* p. 55.
132. Byington, *Jungian Symbolic Psychology.*
133. Carotenuto, *Secret Symmetry.*
134. Ibid., p. 48.
135. Ibid., p.78.
136. Ibid., p.190.
137. Ramos, Denise G. *A Psique do Coração.*
138. Carotenuto, *Secret Symmetry,* p.33.

139. Eugen Bleuler was director of the Burghölzli Mental Hospital when Jung began to work there.

140. Bair, *Jung,* p. 149.

141. Ibid., p. 152.

142. Carotenuto, *Secret Symmetry*, p. 201.

143. Jung, *Red Book*, p. 242, note 115.

144. Jung, *Memories,* p. 180.

145. Bair, *Jung,* p. 387.

146. Jung, *Red Book*, p. 242.

147. Ibid., p. 242, note 118.

148. Ibid., pp. 243f.

149. Ibid., p. 243.

150. Ibid., p. 244.

151. Ibid., p. 243.

152. Ibid., p. 244.

153. Ibid.

154. Ibid.

155. Carotenuto, *Secret Symmetry,* p. 95.

156. Hannah, *Jung.*

157. Bair, *Jung,* p. 387.

158. Shamdasani, Introduction to *Red Book*, p. 202.

159. Jung, *Analytical Psychology,* p. 46.

160. Jung, *Memories,* p. 182.

161. Jung, *Red Book*, p. 246.

162. Jung, *Analytical Psychology*, p. 92.

163. Jung, *Red Book*, p. 247.

164. Ibid., p. 246.

165. Ibid.

166. Ibid., p. 247.

167. Ibid., p. 246.

168. Ibid., p. 247.

169. Ibid., p. 248.

170. Ibid.

171. Ibid.

172. Ibid.

173. Ibid., p. 249.

174. Ibid.

175. Ibid., p. 250.
176. Ibid., p. 251.
177. Ibid., p. 303.
178. Ibid., p. 251.
179. Ibid., pp. 252f.
180. Ibid., p. 253.
181. Ibid., note 227.
182. Ibid., p. 255, note 240.
183. Ibid., p. 254.
184. Ibid., p. 252.
185. Ibid., p. 254.
186. Ibid., p. 305.
187. Jung, *Memories,* p. 248.
188. Jung, *Red Book*, p. 259.
189. Ibid., p. 260.
190. Ibid.
191. Jung, "Children's Dreams: Notes from the Seminar Given in 1936-1940," in Jung. *Red Book*, p. 260, note 12.
192. Jung, *Red Book*, p. 261, note 18.
193. Ibid., p. 262.
194. Ibid.
195. Ibid.
196. Ibid., p. 263.
197. Ibid.
198. Ibid.
199. Ibid, p. 263, note 25.
200. Ibid, p. 330.
201. Ibid.
202. Jung, *Memories,* p. 237.
203. Ibid., pp. 172-173.
204. Ibid., p. 263.
205. Ibid., p. 274.
206. Ibid.
207. Jung, *Red Book*, p. 275.
208. Ibid., pp. 259f.
209. Ibid., pp. 267f.
210. Ibid., p. 276.

211. Ibid.
212. Ibid.
213. Ibid.
214. Shamdasani, Introduction to *Red Book*, p. 275, note 81.
215. Jung, *Red Book*, p. 279.
216. Jung, *Psychological Types*. CW 6, par. 301.
217. Jung, *Red Book*, p. 284.
218. Ibid., p. 286.
219. Ibid., p. 288.
220. Ibid., note 139.
221. Ibid., note 141.
222. Ibid., p. 291.
223. Ibid.
224. Ibid.
225. Ibid., p. 293.
226. Ibid.
227. Ibid., pp. 294f.
228. Ibid., p. 295.
229. Ibid., p. 238.
230. Plato. "Phaedrus", in Shamdasani, Introduction to *Red Book,* p. 238, note 89.
231. Ibid.
232. Jung, *Red Book*, p. 238.
233. Kinsley, David R. *The Divine Player—A Study of Krishna Lila*, p.xii.
234. Zimmer, Heinrich. "Philosophies of India", p. 16.
235. Jung, *Red Book*, p. 295.
236. Ibid., p. 238.
237. Ibid., p. 295.
238. Byington, Carlos A. B. "Teoria Arquetípica".
239. Jung, *Red Book*, p. 295.
240. Ibid.
241. Ibid., p. 297.
242. Ibid., p. 299.
243. Ibid.
244. Shamdasani, Introduction to *Red Book*, p. 299, note 200.
245. Jung, *Answer to Job*. CW 14, par. 741.
246. Jung, *Red Book*, p. 300.

247. Kerényi, Karl. *The Gods of the Greeks*, p. 114.

248. Shamdasani, Introduction to *Red Book*, p. 301, note 211.

249. Jung, C. G. *Red Book*, p. 301.

250. Ibid., p. 304.

251. Ibid.

252. Ibid.

253. Ibid.

254. Ibid.

255. Ibid., p. 310.

256. At this time Jung still had not created the concept of anima, and he equated it to experiencing God (the Self or Central Archetype).

257. Jung, *Red Book*, p. 311.

258. Ibid., p. 312.

259. Ibid., p. 313.

260. Ibid., p. 314.

261. Ibid., p. 315.

262. Ibid.

263. Ibid.

264. Ibid.

265. Ibid., p. 316. About this passage, see the article by Nathan Schwartz-Salant, "The Mark of One Who Has Seen Chaos—A Review of C. G. Jung's Red Book".

266. Jung, *Memories,* p. 191.

267. Paradoxically, it is in the description of the most terrible of wars that one finds the lesson of nonviolence (*ahisma*), and for this reason the *Bhagavad Gita* was Ghandi's bedside reading.

268. Jung, *Red Book*, p. 317.

269. Jung, *The Psychological Aspects of the Kore*. CW 9i, par. 376.

270. Jung, *Red Book*, p. 317.

271. Ibid.

272. Tristan and Isolde represent romantic and adulterous love.

273. Jung, *Red Book*, pp. 317f.

274. Ibid., p. 318.

275. Ibid.

276. Ibid.

277. Ibid., p. 353.

278. Ibid., p. 312.

279. Jung, *Psychology of the Transference*. CW 16, par. 399.

280. Jung, *Red Book*, p. 322.

281. Ibid.

282. Ibid.

283. Bair, *Jung,* p. 731, note 42.

284. Bair, ibid., p. 249.

285. Bair, ibid., p. 250.

286. Jung, *Red Book*, p. 322.

287. Ibid., p. 323.

288. Shamdasani, Introduction to *Red Book*, p. 323, note 320.

289. Jung, *Red Book*, p. 323.

290. Ibid.

291. Ibid.

292. Ibid.

293. Jung had said the same thing to the young girl he met in the castle, in the vision he had on December 28, 1913. See Jung, *Red Book*, p. 263.

294. Ibid., p. 324.

295. Ibid.

296. Ibid.

297. Ibid., p. 325.

298. Ibid., pp. 324f.

299. Ibid., p. 325.

300. Ibid.

301. Ibid.

302. Jung, *Memories,* p. 354.

303. Jung, *Red Book*, p. 326.

304. Ibid.

305. Ibid., p. 327.

306. Ibid.

307. Ibid., p. 326.

308. Ibid., p. 327.

309. Ibid., p. 329.

310. Bair, *Jung*, p. 248.

311. Ibid., p. 730, note 34.

312. Jung, *Memories,* p. 285.

313. Ibid., p. 286.

314. Jung, *Red Book*, p. 365.

315. Ibid., pp. 333f.
316. Ibid., p. 330.
317. Ibid.
318. Ibid. p. 333.
319. Ibid.
320. Ibid.
321. Bair, *Jung,* p. 248.
322. Jung, *Red Book*, p. 334.
323. Ibid.
324. Ibid., p. 335.
325. Ibid.
326. Ibid., p. 231.
327. Ibid.
328. Ibid.
329. Bair, *Jung,* p. 252.
330. Jung, *Red Book,* p. 336.
331. Ibid.
332. Ibid.
333. Ibid., p. 154.
334. McGuire, William and Hull, R. F. C. "C. G. Jung Speaking: Interviews and Encounters", in Jung, *Red Book*, p. 201.
335. Jung, *Red Book*, p. 336.
336. Bair, *Jung,* p. 730, note 39.
337. Hannah, *Jung.*
338. Bair, *Jung,* p. 266.
339. Ibid., p. 390.
340. Ibid., p. 558.
341. Jung, *Memories,* p. 225.
342. van der Post, in Anthony, Maggy, *As Mulheres na Vida de Jung*, p. 59.
343. Jung, *Red Book*, p. 307, note 240.
344. Serrano, Miguel. *C. G. Jung and Hermann Hesse* (This passage translated by Marcelo Corção from the Portuguese *O Círculo Hermético— Hermann Hesse a C. G. Jung,* pp. 76f.).
345. Jung, *Memories,* pp. 353f.

BIBLIOGRAPHIC REFERENCES

Anthony, Maggy. *As mulheres na vida de Jung*. Trans. Constantino Kouzmin-Korovaeff. Rio de Janeiro: Record: Rosa dos Tempos, 1998.

Bair, Deirdre. *Jung: A biography*. 2 vols. New York: Little, Brown and Company, 2003.

Barros, José D'A. "Os trovadores medievais e o amor cortês—reflexões historiográficas." *Revista Aletheia—Estudos sobe Antiguidade e Medievo* 1 (2008): 1.15. Accessed November, 3, 2011.

Bhagavad Gita. Translation and notes by Humberto Rohden. São Paulo: Fundação Alvorada, s/d.

Brandão, Junito de S. *Mitologia Grega*. Petrópolis: Editora Vozes, 1987, 2 v.

Byington, Carlos A. B. "Teoria Arquetípica da História. O Mito Cristão como principal Símbolo Estruturante do Padrão de Alteridade na Cultura Ocidental." *Junguiana—Revista da Sociedade Brasileira de Psicologia Analítica*. 1 (1983): 120.77.

_______. *Jungian Symbolic Psychology*. Evanston, IL: Chiron Publications, 2012.

Carotenuto, Aldo. *A Secret Symmetry—Sabina Spielrein Between Jung and Freud*. New York: Pantheon Books, 1984.

De, S. K. *Early History of the Vaisnava Faith and Movement in Bengal*. Calcutta: Firma K. L. Mukhopadhyay, 1961.

Goethe, Wolfgang. *Faust*. Trans. Bayard Taylor. New York: Houghton Mifflin, 1898.

Guerra, Maria Helena R. M. "Encontro: O Relacionamento Interpessoal Dialético enquanto Símbolo de Totalidade." PhD diss., University of São Paulo, 1988.

Guggenbühl-Craig, Adolph. *Marriage—Dead or Alive?* Zurich: Spring Publications, 1978.

Hannah, Barbara. *Jung: His life and work*. Evanston, IL: Chiron Publications, 1999.

Jung, Carl G. *Red Book*. New York: W. W. Norton, 2009.

_______. *Psychological Types*. CW 6. London: Routledge & Kegan Paul, 1989.

_______. *Analytical Psychology—Notes on the Seminar given in 1925.* Ed. McGuire, W. Princeton: Princeton University Press, 1991.

_______. *The Visions Seminars. From the Complete Notes of Mary Foote.* 2 vols. Zürich: Spring Publications, 1976.

_______. *Psychological Commentary on Kundalini Yoga.* Zürich: Spring, 1976. Lectures three and four.

_______. "Children's Dreams: Notes from the Seminar Given in 1936-1940," in Jung, Carl G., *Red Book.* New York: W. W. Norton, 2009.

_______. *The Psychological Aspects of the Kore.* CW 9i. London: Routledge & Kegan Paul, 1959.

_______. The *Psychology of the Transference.* CW 16. London: Routledge & Kegan Paul, 1954.

_______. *Aion—Researches into the Phenomenology of the Self.* CW 9ii. Princeton: Princeton University Press, 1979.

_______. *Answer to Job.* CW 14. London: Routledge & Kegan Paul, 1958.

_______. *Memories, Dreams, Reflections.* New York: Random House, 1989.

Jung, Emma, and Von Franz, Marie-Louise. *The Grail Legend.* New York: C. G. Jung Foundation for Analytical Psychology, 1970.

Kerényi, Karl. *Dionysos—Archetypal Image of Indestructible Life.* Princeton: Princeton University Press, 1976.

_______. *The Gods of the Greeks.* Surrey, UK: Thames and Hudson, 1979.

Kinsley, David R. *The Divine Player—A Study of Krishna Lila.* Delhi: Motilal Banarsidass, 1979.

McGuire, William., ed. *The Freud/Jung Letters: The Correspondence Between Sigmund Freud and C. G. Jung.* London: Penguin Books, 1991.

McGuire, William, and Hull, R. F. C., eds. "C. G. Jung Speaking: Interviews and Encounters." in Shamdasani, Sonu. Introduction to the *Red Book*, New York: W. W. Norton, 2009.

New American Standard Bible. California: Lockman Foundation, 1977.

Ramos, Denise G. *A Psique do Coração.* São Paulo: Cultrix, 1995.

Schwartz-Salant, Nathan. "The Mark of One Who Has Seen Chaos: A Review of C. G. Jung's Red Book." *Quadrant, Journal of the C. G. Jung Foundation for Analytical Psychology.* XXXX:2 (2010): 11-38.

Serrano, Miguel. *O Círculo Hermético—Hermann Hesse a C. G. Jung*. Trans. Marcelo Corção. São Paulo: Editora Brasiliense, 1973.

Shamdasani, Sonu. Introduction to Jung's *Red Book*. New York: W. W. Norton, 2009.

Zimmer, Heinrich R. *Philosophies of India.* Ed. Joseph Campbell. Princeton: Princeton University Press, 1989.

INDEX

Maria Helena Mandacarú Guerra

Psychologist - graduated in 1976 (Catholic University of São Paulo – Specialization in Jungian psychotherapy - graduated in 1980 (Catholic University of São Paulo - PUC-SP);

Master in Clinical Psychology - graduated in 1988 (Institute of Psychology - University of São Paulo);

Teacher of Analytical Psychology in Sedes Sapientiae Institute (São Paulo) since 1982.

Editor of *Jung & Body* – Journal of the Specialization Course in Analytical Psychology and Body Techniques in Sedes Sapientiae Institute (São Paulo) since 2001 until today.

Author of many articles on Analytical Psychology.

Lecturer at all Jungian Latin-American Congresses since 1998.

Photo of the author by Dani Mandacarú.

Also in this Series, by Daryl Sharp

Please see last page for discounts and postage/handling.

THE SECRET RAVEN

Conflict and Transformation in the Life of Franz Kafka

ISBN 978-0-919123-00-7. (1980) 128 pp. $25

PERSONALITY TYPES: Jung's Model of Typology

ISBN 978-0-919123-30-9. (1987) 128 pp. **Diagrams** $25

THE SURVIVAL PAPERS: Anatomy of a Midlife Crisis + DEAR GLDYS

2 books. ISBN 978-0-919123-34-2/36-6. (1988-89) 160/144 pp. $25 each

JUNG LEXICON: A Primer of Terms and Concepts

ISBN 978-0-919123-48-9. (1991) 160 pp. **Diagrams** $25

GETTING TO KNOW YOU: The Inside Out of Relationship

ISBN 978-0-919123-56-4. (1992) 128 pp. $25

THE BRILLIG TRILOGY:

1. **CHICKEN LITTLE: The Inside Story** ***(A Jungian romance)***
   ISBN 978-0-919123-62-5. (1993) 128 pp. $25
2. **WHO AM I, REALLY? Personality, Soul and Individuation**
   ISBN 978-0-919123-68-7. (1995) 144 pp. $25
3. **LIVING JUNG: The Good and the Better**
   ISBN 978-0-919123-73-1. (1996) 128 pp. $25

JUNGIAN PSYCHOLOGY UNPLUGGED: My Life As an Elephant

ISBN 978-0-919123-81-6. (1998) 160 pp. $25

DIGESTING JUNG: Food for the Journey

ISBN 978-0-919123-96-0. (2001) 128 pp. $25

JUNG UNCORKED: Rare Vintages from the Cellar of Analytical Psychology

4 books. ISBN 978-1-894574-21-1/22-8/24-2/27-3 (2008-9) 128 pp. each. $25 each

THE SLEEPNOT TRILOGY:

1. **NOT THE BIG SLEEP: On having fun, seriously** ***(A Jungian romance)***
   ISBN 978-0-894574-13-6. (2005) 128 pp. $25
2. **ON STAYING AWAKE: Getting Older and Bolder** *(Another Jungian romance)*
   ISBN 978-0-894574-16-7. (2006) 144 pp. $25
3. **EYES WIDE OPEN: Late Thoughts** *(Another Jungian romance)*
   ISBN 978-0-894574-18-1.. (2007) 160 pp. $25

Books by Edward F. Edinger in this Series

SCIENCE OF THE SOUL: A Jungian Perspective
ISBN 978-1-894574-03-6. (2002) 128 pp. $25

THE PSYCHE ON STAGE
Individuation Motifs in Shakespeare and Sophocles
ISBN 978-0-919123-94-6. (2001) 96 pp. **Illustrated** $25

EGO AND SELF: The Old Testament Prophets
ISBN 978-0-919123-91-5. (2000) 160 pp. $25

THE PSYCHE IN ANTIQUITY
Book 1: Early Greek Philosophy
ISBN 978-0-919123-86-1. (1999) 128 pp. $25
Book 2: Gnosticism and Early Christianity
ISBN 978-0-919123-87-8. (1999) 160 pp. $25

THE AION LECTURES: Exploring the Self in Jung's *Aion*
ISBN 978-0-919123-72-4. (1996) 208 pp. **30 illustrations** $30

MELVILLE'S MOBY-DICK: An American Nekyia
ISBN 978-0-919123-70-0. (1995) 160 pp. $25

THE MYSTERIUM LECTURES
A Journey Through Jung's *Mysterium Coniunctionis*
ISBN 978-0-919123-66-3. (1995) 352 pp. **90 illustrations** $40

THE MYSTERY OF THE CONIUNCTIO
Alchemical Image of Individuation
ISBN 978-0-919123-67-6. (1994) 112 pp. **48 illustrations** $25

THE CHRISTIAN ARCHETYPE A Jungian Commentary on the Life of Christ
ISBN 978-0-919123-27-4. (1987) 144 pp. **34 illustrations** $25

THE BIBLE AND THE PSYCHE
Individuation Symbolism in the Old Testament
ISBN 978-0-919123-23-1. (1986) 176 pp. $30

ENCOUNTER WITH THE SELF
A Jungian Commentary on William Blake's *Illustrations of the Book of Job*
ISBN 978-0-919123-21-2. (1986) 80 pp. **22 illustrations** $25

THE CREATION OF CONSCIOUSNESS
Jung's Myth for Modern Man
ISBN 978-0-919123-13-7. (1984) 128 pp. **10 illustrations** $25

Also in this Series, by Marie-Louise von Franz

AURORA CONSURGENS: On the Problem of Opposites in Alchemy
ISBN 978-0-919123-90-8. (2000) 576pp. **30-page Index *Sewn*** $50
A penetrating commentary on a rare medieval treatise, scattered throughout with insights relevant to the process of individuation in modern men and women.

THE PROBLEM OF THE PUER AETERNUS
ISBN 978-0-919123-88-5. (2000) 288pp. **11 illustrations *Sewn*** $40
The term *puer aeternus* (Latin, eternal youth) is used in Jungian psychology to describe a certain type of man or woman: charming, creative, and ever in pursuit of their dreams. This is the classic study of those who remain adolescent well into their adult years.

THE CAT: A Tale of Feminine Redemption
ISBN 978-0-919123-84-7. (1999) 128pp. **8 illustrations *Sewn*** $25
"The Cat" is a Romanian fairy tale about a princess who at the age of seventeen is bewitched—turned into a cat. . . . One by one von Franz unravels the symbolic threads.

C.G. JUNG: His Myth in Our Time
ISBN 978-0-919123-78-6. (1998) 368pp. **30-page Index** *Sewn* $40
The most authoritative biography of Jung, comprising an historical account of his seminal ideas, including his views on the collective unconscious, archetypes and complexes, typology, creativity, active imagination and individuation.

ARCHETYPAL PATTERNS IN FAIRY TALES
ISBN 978-0-919123-77-9. (1997) 192pp. *Sewn* $30
In-depth studies of six fairy tales—from Spain, Denmark, China, France and Africa, and one from the Grimm collection—with references to parallel themes in many others.

REDEMPTION MOTIFS IN FAIRY TALES
ISBN 978-0-919123-01-4. (1980) 128pp. *Sewn* $25
A nonlinear approach to the significance of fairy tales for an understanding of the process of psychological development. Concise explanations of complexes, projection, archetypes and active imagination. A modern classic.

ON DIVINATION AND SYNCHRONICITY
The Psychology of Meaningful Chance
ISBN 978-0-919123-02-1. (1980) 128pp. **15 illustrations** *Sewn* $25
A penetrating study of the psychological aspects of time, number and methods of divining fate such as the I Ching, astrology, Tarot, palmistry, dice, etc.

ALCHEMY: An Introduction to the Symbolism and the Psychology
ISBN 978-0-919123-04-5. (1980) 288pp. **84 illustrations** *Sewn* $40